OLD TIMERS

DAVID DARCY

OLD TIMERS

Stories about the good old days

MURDOCH BOOKS

CONTENTS

INTRODUCTION 6

THE WONDER YEARS 8

TWO PEAS IN A POD 54

ONE & THREEPENCE A WEEK 88

ALL ROADS LEAD HOME 120

INTRODUCTION

A hundred years ago, life in Australia was very, very different. Horses and carts were the main form of transport. It was a time before motorcars ruled the streets. Information was shared through letters, delivered officially by telegram, or run up the street by children in short handwritten notes. There was no email. No internet. Few phones.

There was no electricity at the flick of a switch. No refrigeration with the push of a plug. There was no iPod, iPhone or Facebook. And there was certainly no TV. Kids made do with what they had. They occupied themselves with simple games, like marbles, a skipping rope, or two tin cans and a piece of string.

It was a time when children were familiar with life's basic skills. They helped grow and cultivate vegetables in the garden, they carted water, they chopped wood, they did their chores—lots of chores. Rural kids could milk a cow, separate the cream and turn the butter if needed—all before going to school in the morning.

Joyce from Allora (page 22) was one such kid. When it comes to her childhood, she has a swag of great memories, from swinging off willow trees down by the creek to yoking the horses and riding one, two or three on the back, off to school in the morning. She relives her childhood memories with great fondness, enthusiasm and hilarity.

But not everyone had it good as a kid. A hundred years ago, life changed so dramatically for Edna (page 28) that her story is hard to believe. Motherless, left with strangers and her siblings taken away, her childhood became a living nightmare. Tossed from pillar to post, unloved and unwanted, she scratched out an existence in doorways and basements, amongst the rats, cockroaches and dogs that she slept next to. It's a lonesome, tragic tale, but somehow Edna found strength.

Life stories can be heartbreaking, to say the least. But they can also be inspiring, joyous and enriching. There's a lot to be gained listening to an older generation talk about the moments that make up their lives—hearing stories of their youth and walking barefooted to school, riding a billy cart to the local shop or leaving school at 14 to get a job.

Although her father was uneducated in the formal sense, Bess is proud of her dad (page 48). Taught to read by his mother in the Clarence River goldfields of the mid 1800s, Bess's dad taught her the values she's carried with her her whole life—values of general decency and to treat others as you'd want to be treated yourself. Her recollections about the Great Depression vary wildly from her urban peers. While city children knew hardship and hunger, the rich farm life her parents provided meant the Depression left Bess largely unscathed.

Then there's Ray (page 148). He's been keeping bees for more than 80 years. He has an enormous wealth of knowledge, passed down from generation to generation by his forefathers, and today passed on to his son. Add to this, season after season, decade upon decade, of first-hand experience working in the Australian bush. An unassuming gentleman, unperturbed by accolades, riches or notoriety, Ray's story reads like an MGM classic—raging rivers and angry bee swarms—and success against the odds.

These people helped shape this nation. Looking back they lived through tough, character-building times. They were resilient. They had to be. They faced the despair of the Depression and the uncertainty of world wars.

When World War II broke out, some 20,000 women joined the Australian Women's Army Service to help relieve men of certain military roles. At 18 years of age, Daph signed up to defend the country she so proudly calls home (page 92). Facing some bewilderment and resentment from male officers, she nevertheless forged a remarkable military career, doing top secret work and operating some of the earliest computers—tracking air force and navy courses.

And when this generation weren't working or defending the country, they let their hair down at the local dance. The dance was the social pinnacle for many communities, and the be all and end all to a great weekend. Aub will testify to that (page 56).

Kay met Barrie at a dance (page 82). Her journey was full of twists and turns, the good, the bad and the forlorn. Unlucky in love on the first two occasions, it would seem she hit the jackpot third time around. Love isn't rocket science, but in her case, it played a part.

But not all love stories have a happy ending, especially during times of war. Bonnie (page 68) has kept a secret close to her heart for 70 years. She only need look at you through those heartbroken eyes and say the words 'If only' to make the tears roll down your cheeks.

These lives have been filled with the ups and downs, highs and lows, good and bad that we all must face. And after a lifetime experiencing all that the world had to offer, for many this has also meant returning to the place they first called home.

Long gone is the smell of freshly baked buns from the local bakery, the happy hellos from the butcher or the sounds of small children playing games at sunset up and down the main street of Yongala. For Yvonne (page 156), all that's left are loving memories.

Old Timers is a collection of honest, personal, inspiring and engaging life moments from a bygone era. These stories are from a range of people, from all walks of life. They reflect a time and a place in Australian history.

Bess (far right) with her mother, Sarah, and siblings, Agnes, Daphne and Charlie. (See page 48.)

THE WONDER YEARS

MARY 'SHARPIE'
FROM DALVEEN
BORN IN STANTHORPE, 1928

Where I lived in Stanthorpe as a kid there was only a dirt road and no electricity. It was 1939 when the power came to town.

My mother was a good cook. We'd all sit around the table in the morning before we went to school and we'd have porridge, then we'd have bacon and eggs or whatever was on the menu. Then we'd take our lunch to school. Then we'd come home and Mum would cook a big tea of a night, and we'd all bog in again. There was always plenty to eat. And plenty of milk to drink. It was good!

The swaggies used to come around. They'd come down to my mother's house in Stanthorpe, near the railway line, and they would bring their billy cans. Mum would give them tea and a bit of bread, and us kids would follow the swaggies up onto the railway line and talk to them until the train come. They'd hop on the hopper and away they'd go.

I was about 15 when I went to the city and I was so amazed. I had rides on the trams and then they took me to the beach and I'd never seen so much water in me life! I'd never been away from the bush before.

But they were the good old days, you know. And we can't bring the good old days back. It's all technology and different stuff today and we just have to go on living with it. All that's left is the memories.

One day my mother told me to go down to Mr Sheen's butcher shop and get a pound of sausages. So I walked into the shop and said, 'Good morning, Mr Sheen.' 'Mary, what do want?' 'My mother said a pound of beef sausages, thank you, Mr Sheen. And I don't want those ones you've been hosing the maggots off, up there on the rail.' He looked at me and he said, 'You're the cheekiest girl I've ever known!'

I remember having one of those celluloid dolls. If you got a dint in it, you just had to suck the dint out.

I remember Mum used to knit and sew. I started knitting in the Fourth Grade, I think. I was only about eight or nine. I used to like knitting. We were knitting scarves for soldiers [during World War II]—I remember it was an odd stitch—and as I got older I used to knit balaclavas and things at school. Yes, I remember making scarves for the soldiers.

Mum started us doing things for our box. Because if you're gunna get married you had to have a glory box. So we started doing fancy work, crochet and things like that. Mum taught us all that.

BETTY
FROM COLAC

BORN IN COLAC, 1930

VIC · 3250

MARGARET
FROM KALLANGUR

BORN IN MELBOURNE, 1931

I had two older brothers. We used to play football and marbles. I liked playing with them because it taught me how to look after myself.

I remember walking up to the corner shop, getting something for Mum. I used to get a loaf of bread or milk, or deliver a message or something. It was just down the street a little way. There was a lolly shop and a grocery shop at the end of our street.

Sometimes I'd take the boys' truck—a little truck that my father made for them. It was just a box on wheels with a thing sticking out the back so you could put one foot out and scoot along, and it had a rope for steering on the two front wheels.

I remember Saturday morning I did chores. I had to help sweep the house or hang washing out. Things like that. Or help Mum in the kitchen. That's all Mum ever did. Bake—bake biscuits and cakes. She was a very good cook.

My father used to amuse us with this Mickey Mouse doll when we were growing up. It was just an old-fashioned hand puppet. I found it in the cupboard again recently.

I can recall our Ford T car—a brand new 1925 model. I can still see that radiator with the word 'Ford' on it.

I was a Depression kid, so we didn't have much money. I can remember I'd play spinning tops and marbles, and we used to flick cards on the wall.

ROBERT
FROM PERTH

WA · 6000

BORN IN KATANNING, 1922

I remember when I was about five, I was taught to milk cows on the dairy. We had two crushers. Cows on each side. And I remember I just got into milking cows. I milked cows for years and years and years. I went to school at Inverramsay but we also worked on the farm. We had to work on the farm!

We used to have draught horses—there were no signs of tractors in those days. We had to yoke those draught horses up. And we had a sulky, of course. We didn't have a car at all. Then our father would load up the cream—those big cream cans. We used to have to take the cream about two miles down to the station on the way to school. The men would lift it off the sulky and then we'd go on to school. Yes, we'd get up and milk the cows, yoke the horses, take the horses back and unyoke them, then go to school. We didn't have to do that every day. The train only came out three days a week, so we did it three days a week.

JOYCE
FROM ALLORA
BORN IN WARWICK, 1927

I can remember going to school barefoot with the frost on the ground. And I can remember this as if it was yesterday … I was about six and I ran under the steps at school and I split my head open. There was no phone or car, so the teacher stopped a bloke that was going to town. He lived near the school. Anyway, I can remember going to Dr Tremaine in town. Well, he stitched it up, and the fella, Bob Doogle, that drove me to town, he drove me home again. We didn't have any way of contacting anyone. There wasn't any phones. So I went to school and then come home with a stitched-up head. Those were the days! Mum was a bit shocked.

> I've always grown my own vegetables. That's because we had to when we were kids. We never, ever bought vegetables. We had a great big vegetable garden down near the creek. I often think back to when I was a kid—how much I enjoyed this and enjoyed that.

For entertainment we used to go down the creek and swing on the willow trees. Or we used to put jam tins in the creek when it was only yay high, and we'd catch the crabs. Oh, we loved crabbing! You'd put the tins in the creek in the morning and go down in the afternoon and get your crabs. Take 'em home, boil 'em up and 'eat em.

We'd make our own entertainment. Nobody had time to entertain all these kids. There were berry trees that used to grow along the creek and we'd pick those berries and make necklaces and bangles. We thought that was just lovely.

We didn't have dolls. I remember somebody gave us a case of mangoes. We ate the mangoes, then we scrubbed the fur up on the seed to make hair and then we painted a face. That was a doll. We thought that was just lovely. We didn't care about bought dolls, we didn't even know about such a thing in those days.

In winter, we had a bath in front of the fire—in the big washing tubs, two at a time in the tub. I can still remember kicking around in that water, then jumping into bed. We used to sleep two in a bed, sometimes three. At Christmas time, we put the stocking on the end of our bed—we only got things that we needed, like a hat or socks or a belt, then there might be a few home-made lollies and a piece of fruit. That was so much fun. Everything was fun!

I wish everybody could experience the life that I had. I do, I really do. Because then they'd appreciate everything. I say that all the time—I am really pleased the way I was brought up. I'd hate to be rearing a family today, there's no discipline. My childhood was good training and I wouldn't have wanted to be brought up any other way.

We used to walk to town in them times, but it's different now. The town was small then. There wasn't much at all. Just a store, post office, police station, that's all. Not many cars—they used to have them horse and sulkies, sometimes a buggy and two horses. That's in the good old days.

GLADYS
FROM WILCANNIA

BORN IN WILCANNIA, 1926

I been here a long time. I was born down there on the bank of the river, down behind the old hospital. An Aboriginal woman brought me into this world down there. We went to Pooncarie then. That's where my family really come from. That's where I grew up. I started school in Pooncarie. School was alright. Then we went to Menindee.

I don't know how old I was when they moved us there. White man there, manager, Mr Parks, he was the manager, see. Mr Blacksure, he was the school teacher. There was a good few kids in the school. There's only one left, me mate Doris, who's in home care.

There were just us dark kids. It was on a mission, an Aboriginal mission. We used to fight with the other ones, then we'd all be mates again. You know what kids were like in them days. We used to play with the bat and the ball, and catches.

It was hot at school, but it never used to worry us. Heat never used to worry us—go for swim then, in the river. One time we swam across, me and my brother—the river was rising. They said, 'Go upstream!' So we went upstream. Where we landed was right in front of where our mother was. She pulled us out and give us a hiding then. She put the strap around us.

There was a lot of water in the river back then. We used to have a bucket at the river—wind it down and then get the water, and carry the bucket home, see. Nothing like today.

EDNA
FROM GOSFORD

BORN IN SYDNEY, 1911

People don't know what I went through. They just don't understand.

I was four and a half when my mother got sick. We used to live in St Peters. Next to the railway. In the houses, upstairs. She was sick in bed with a newborn. The baby was very ill. They took Mum to hospital and someone took the baby. She got worse in the hospital and she died.

I had a baby brother and I also had a younger sister, and an older sister, who was about ten—she was a cripple and she couldn't speak. Her name was Vera.

I was five. I can remember the day like it was yesterday. I was five the day my mother was buried. The lady where I was staying had a daughter who was about 14. She put a big bow in my hair and a big bow on the back of my dress.

But life changed after Mum died. Life really changed. My younger sister must have got a permanent place somewhere, I don't know. We all went different ways. I was just a child so I didn't know where they went.

The father wasn't much of a father. After my mother died, my father left me with people. He didn't care. First, he left me with this lady—I used to have to sleep in the corner, on the floor in the corner—but she died. But that's how it was. Everyone was sick in the street.

There was the epidemic, a flu epidemic. They were all dying. That was terrible to see. I was just a little girl. I would stand on a chair or a box and look out the window. We didn't have cars or anything. And I could see the people in boxes in the back of carts. People were being wheeled down the streets in wheelbarrows and on carts. Taken away to die. We stood there and got a drop of sugar and eucalyptus on our tongue. For prevention. People didn't know any better.

The war was on [World War I] and times were tough. I got shifted from house to house. Sleeping where I could, eating whatever I could. I was like a street kid. My dad was nowhere to be seen. I never had a toy, I never had one. I never saw my sisters and brother after Mum died, so I had nobody. I never had a childhood. I never played in the streets. I never went to school. I never had anything like that. No Christmas. I was always minding people's children or running messages, or something like that. They just pushed me around from one place to another, around the train lines at St Peters. That's all I knew. It's a wonder I wasn't shovelled out with the garbage.

I was given a plate and a message. When I was five or six I had to go to the butcher and get the meat. I couldn't even count. They let a little kid like me mind children and run to the shops. I used to have to go to the bakery. I had no shoes and it was so cold. I used to lean up against the bakery wall because it was warm. I used to take the bread home, then the women would make the sandwiches, then I'd take the sandwiches to the men in the brickyard. No shoes on my poor little feet. I used to have to walk on all the broken bricks. My poor little feet always had brick bits in them. Cut and sore.

When I look back I don't know how I managed. But, I suppose I wasn't the only one. When I look back I wouldn't dare let my children do this. I wouldn't dare. When I think back, I think there were some nasty people who had no heart.

> I remember this day. My mother was only thin and she had a hat on. She was going to church, had a Bible in one hand and her hat on. She looked lovely. I've still got her Bible.

When I used to get upset about my mother, I used to go in a real dark corner and have a cry. And I'd see her; I'd feel she was there somewhere, somewhere in the room, but I didn't find her, of course.

I'll tell you this—I shouldn't tell you because you might think I'm trying to show off—when Mum had the baby, the nurses used to come and help turn the baby and fix them up and give the mother a bit of a treatment and that. Anyway, we lived in this small house upstairs. You went down the stairs to the laundry, there was a copper and all the families shared the laundry.

Anyway, this day I went down to do something in the laundry and I saw this dirty nappy. This little baby's dirty nappy. So I got up on a chair and started scrubbing and cleaning it in the tub. There I was scrubbing and scrubbing, and, this was true, all of a sudden I'm on a chair and I thought I was going to fall because one of the nurses had come up from behind and put her arms around me. She must have got upset. I thought she was gunna go crook at me. But she must have seen what I was doing. I was only a child. I guess it would make you cry, seeing a little girl cleaning nappies.

⁂

Down one of these streets they used to sell rabbits. You could buy a fresh killed rabbit. Anyway, my father took me to this place and the woman said she didn't want me, but he left me there anyway. I just slept on the ground there. My chore was I had to put the skins out on a piece of tin. I used to feel sick. The smell of rabbits. My father didn't even know them, but he left me there. I used to

Edna with her husband, Joe, in happy times.

sleep where the dog was, underneath the house. I never saw the father, but the woman came down one day and gave me a sandwich. She never wanted me there. So she gave me this sandwich and took me back across the tramlines. She found my father and said, 'I don't want her, I don't want her!' I suppose my father thought, 'If I leave her there, she'll keep her.' But she didn't want me.

The last lady I lived with, before I met my husband, she was a horrible woman. My husband, Joe, had happened to come and stay with a relation, in a house on the other side of the street. My husband came over and told her off. He saw what I was getting to eat and said 'I could get better food at the dump!' He used to walk me home from the train. Oh, how silly love is! He was a good man. I never had a nice dress. I never had nice clothes—not until I met him and got married.

Anyway, so that was my childhood. No toys, only some rubbish. But never mind. The good fairies helped me. That's the way it went.

I get sad thinking if my mother had lived, I would probably have had a dolly. I probably would have played with my brother and sisters and had a childhood. But that's not her fault.

I don't know, sometimes ... I remember seeing my mother, before she died. She came down the stairs with a hat and a prayer book in her hand. She was going to church. I don't think the church was far away. I never forgot her. But, I do wonder, why didn't God help her a bit more? Just give her a little bit more time. He must have had a reason.

There were times when I thought life wasn't worth living. Nobody liked me. Nobody loved me. And I had no one to look after me. No home, no mother, nothing. That's when I didn't want to live. But when you get a little bit of kindness, something happens, life changes completely. You can find the best life if you look after it.

I've had my ups and downs, but you never get anything for free, you have to fight for it and then hold onto it.

I worked with Dad on the oyster farms through the Great Depression, but we never went hungry. Dad was a provider.

Dad was a great gardener and a great builder. In fact, Dad could build anything. He built coffins out of cedar and was the undertaker for his uncle, Ned Davis. He built a lot of small boats, houses and bridges.

On one occasion, he was working on the Toorooka Bridge and on Christmas Eve he decided to walk home. He walked all night with the dingoes following and howling. He got home to find that everyone had gone across the river to Fig Tree. Being a bit hungry, he boiled nine eggs—left the shells behind as evidence—went across the river to Fig Tree, had dinner with everyone and then left to walk back to Toorooka.

TED FROM MACKSVILLE

BORN IN NAMBUCCA HEADS, 1913

Regattas were a big event in the old days. My dad was a rower. In fact, he beat the champ once, Mr Saul, on a tummy full of watermelon.

The Wonder Years

MAY FROM LITTLEHAMPTON

PLACE OF BIRTH UNKNOWN, 1918

I couldn't ride a bike, so I walked everywhere. I tried to ride a horse once. No thank you! I'm frightened of those big things. No, I was happy walking. We used to walk to school on the back roads. And I remember them putting the second road through town. One up and one down. I can remember seeing the men working on the roads with picks and shovels—it was hard work. We used to walk along Maple Street, down Ayres Hill Road and down past the blacksmith shop on the corner.

We used to get a penny every Saturday and Mum would walk us to the lolly store. And you'd get the tray and you'd pick out what you wanted off the tray. That was your treat at the weekend. At Christmas we used to hang our stocking at the end of the bed—you might get a banana, an orange and an apple, with a small present on top. 'Oh, Mum! Father Christmas has been!'

Mum used to make our dresses with a hand-cranked sewing machine. We'd stand there and be fitted. I used to sing at the Congregational Church anniversary. So I always had a new dress for that.

We used to pick blackberries and Mum would make bread and blackberry jam and scalded cream for afternoon tea. It's a wonder we weren't this size! Mum used to do all her cooking on the wood stove. We used to have to pick the sticks up in the morning so Dad could light the fire and boil the kettle, and we could have a meal.

I remember the electricity being put on. We had a light outside and I remember it getting flicked on for the first time. It was a big deal back then.

My sister passed away during the war [World War II]. We were in a bomb shelter hiding from the bombs, in a train tunnel—very deep in the tunnel. I was four years old and Mum was holding my hand. My sister was playing with some other girls—they played 'Ring a Ring o' Roses' and a bomb dropped outside. A long way away. A piece of shrapnel flew all the way up the tunnel. It missed hundreds of other people and it hit my sister ...

VINCENZINA
FROM FREMANTLE

BORN IN ITALY, 1939

I remember her face ... I remember. She died. That's my first memory. I never forget 16 August 1944.

JEAN
FROM NIMBIN

BORN IN APSLEY, 1915

I learnt to ride a horse between the ages of three and five. My two older brothers and I used to ride a horse to school every day. All three of us, bareback.

We went to a little country school, which would have been about two or three miles from where we were living at Edenville, a district out near Kyogle. We used to ride a horse every day and leave it in the horse paddock at the school.

We had a great time at school, we really did. We had a good teacher. There would have been 30 kids at the school—the families were a bit bigger in those days. Some children didn't start school until they were seven, because they were too small to go the distance if they didn't have a horse to ride.

We all went barefooted. I didn't wear shoes to school until I was nearly 12—when I had to go to high school. That meant I had to go into town, so I had to wear shoes because everybody else did.

When I went to high school I was one of the first students that sat for the intermediate exam in Kyogle in 1930—when I was 15. There weren't that many children that went that far. You could leave school at 14 and most of the kids lived on farms and they were needed at home. So I was lucky enough to be allowed to go to school until I was 15 and do the exam.

Jean (right) with her sister Margaret 'Peggy' in their Sunday best.

I have vague memories from when I was three, of seeing a soldier come home from the 1918 war. I was intrigued by the clothes he was wearing, because he was still in his uniform. That was something I hadn't seen before—my father didn't go to the war.

NELL
FROM SADDLEWORTH

BORN IN AUBURN, 1930

Well, my uncle and aunty, who lived out of town here, had four children. Three of them died of tuberculosis. They took a trip over to New Zealand and back to get away, but when they got back they couldn't settle. So they said they'd go on another trip. And they came to see my father and said, 'What about it? Do you want to come?' My dad liked to travel, so he said yes and decided to take his whole family around the world.

It was autumn 1939 when we left on a big ship from Adelaide to Perth, then to Colombo. We drove from Colombo to Kandy. It rained a lot and it was very wet. There where lots of little naked children on the side of the road.

At Bombay [Mumbai], all the children used to hang around the car wanting money. The driver would throw pennies out the window. That still goes on today. Yes, there were a lot of poor people around, but it was very interesting.

Then we went to Aden and to the Red Sea. We drove to Cairo and saw the pyramids and Tutankhamun. I didn't know about all that. It wasn't till later at school when we learnt about all the history, and I said, 'I'd seen all that.'

Then we went for our trip around Europe—Italy, France. When we went to Versailles, in France, I stayed in the bus. Fancy missing out on Versailles! Switzerland, we went up into the mountains. That was the first time I'd seen snow. Then back to England and a tour around. I remember we saw a panda at the zoo, sitting in a chair feeding itself. And we went to see Shirley Temple at the pictures.

Then we got on the *Queen Mary* to go over to New York—a few days in New York, which was interesting. You could go to the drug stores to get sandwiches. I didn't mind them, so long as they didn't have mayonnaise on them. Then Niagara Falls and over to Chicago ... Jasper ... Victoria Island and then down the coast to San Francisco. Then Yosemite. That was beautiful. At Los Angeles we got back on a ship to Hawaii, Fiji, New Zealand. Then while we were headed home from Auckland to Sydney, war was declared [World War II]. So the ship was in total darkness, even no smoking on deck ... then back to Adelaide.

When we got home, we had to go back to school for a month to finish off the year. My sister came last and I came second last—well, we hadn't had much schooling! I remember the first day on the boat my mother got out all the school books and we looked at them. That was the first and last time we saw those books.

A friend of mine from school days has still got a letter I wrote her when I was travelling 76 years ago. She's kept it. And one of my friends at college said that I'd been pointed out to her as 'the girl who went around the world'.

My parents moved out here from Sydney in 1930 to escape the Great Depression. When they got the land it was just a mass of rabbits and prickly pear and rubbish. No facilities, no electricity, no telephone, no water. They raised six kids of which I'm the eldest. Four boys and two girls. The only school out here was a little school, but you couldn't get past primary. So we went to Sydney schools. They were pretty primitive times, just after the war [World War II].

NSW · 2850

JOHN
FROM HILL END

BORN IN SYDNEY, 1932

If you went to boarding school, you virtually lived on army tucker.

The Wonder Years **47**

BESS
FROM GLENREAGH
BORN IN SOUTH GRAFTON, 1922

I can recall my brother piggy-backing me around the creek, up Tallawudjah Creek, under the orange trees. We had a grove of orange trees. I was the middle child in the family and I was known as the runt of the litter. My sister was two years younger than me, but I can't remember ever being bigger than her. I remember the teacher at school used to think we were twins.

Looking back, we had a marvellous childhood. I don't ever remember being bored. We played outside all the time. We had loving parents—a father that told us stories around the fire at night and a mother that cooked everything we wanted. But when I look back now, I don't remember butcher's meat, only corned meat, because we were about 11 miles from the nearest shop. So it was ... I cringe now when I think about it ... the wildlife that we ate. Pigeons, scrub birds, wild turkeys. Now I have wild turkeys come here to visit me. I think it's my dad come back to haunt me.

There was fish in the creek. There was veggies in the garden. There was always plenty to eat. I remember after I was married, my husband kept talking about the Depression. I asked him one day what was he talking about? He'd been reared by his mum in Moss Vale, in a town, and he could remember being hungry as a kid. Here we were, about the same age, and I couldn't ever remember being hungry in my life.

Mum had a big garden. We carried water from the creek. We had no water laid on, of course. And you took your washing to the creek and you played by the creek while Mum did the washing. It was easier to carry the washing to the creek than it was to carry the water to the house.

We had hand-me-downs from our cousins. I don't ever remember having new clothes. Mum sewed, so we always wore something that had been cut down and remade. We were poor, but we didn't know we were poor, because nobody at school had shoes or fancy clothes; there was no such thing as a uniform.

Dad was always pulling the wool with us kids. We didn't know there wasn't a Santa Claus until I was about 13 or 14. We couldn't believe it, because Dad told such wild stories about Santa Claus. He used to run through the house with a bell and stuff. Dad used to hang a big chaff bag where he slept and he used to say because he had a big bag, he'd get all the presents. And we firmly believed him. Oh, he'd have us on!

Dad never went to school a day in his life, but he could read. He was reared in the goldfields up the head of the

Bess (second from right) with her siblings, Daphne, Charlie and Agnes, in the citrus orchard at their grandparents' property in 1925.

Clarence River. He was taught to read by his mother. Even though he wasn't educated in the formal sense, he knew about life and he taught us about life. And that was an inspiration to us, to all his family.

The creek crossed the road three times on the way to school. We'd always dawdle on the way home, till the dingoes started howling. I remember we used to go and light fires and burn stumps at night to keep the dingoes away—they used to come in and kill the calves. I remember hearing the dingoes howling, and having goosebumps and being scared. I used to go with Dad and lay out the dingo baits and he'd get as many as 8 or 9 in a night. I'd help him skin them. I only had one brother and he couldn't stand the sight of blood. But I didn't mind. I must have been a bloodthirsty little kid.

Dad had a soldier's settlement, about 468 acres. I think the bank owned it more than he did. He did sell out later on. The house is not there anymore.

We decided to move to my grandmother's farm, between here and Nana Glen. Then we went share farming down the Clarence River. It was the war years [World War II], but we had a great social life. During those years a lot of soldiers left our district and I had a lot of pen friends. I had about 17 pen friends.

Tallawudjah Creek

The creek is still lazily flowing along
But where is my playground of youth?
The one-room school, like the settlers, has gone
And the road has a different route.

And the shadows that danced on the white-washed walls
As I played by the firelight's glare
Like the spirit and folk of that era have gone
But the creek of my youth is still there.

By Bess

I was milking 24 cows of a morning, by hand, as a young girl, to help a neighbour out and I got sick. I got mumps. So Mum and Dad decided that I couldn't do that job any more. I'd lost about a stone and I couldn't afford to lose any more, so they decided I needed to go away, have a month's holiday. So they sent me on the train to Wyrallah, near Lismore. I stayed there a month and had a wonderful time.

Coming home, the train broke down, this side of Casino. I was headed back to Grafton. I was in a dog box and there was this fella sitting beside me, and two other people. I didn't know this at the time but he was 'jumping the rattler' – that's what they used to call it in those days if you didn't have a ticket. I learnt all this out later. Anyway, my host family had given me a bag of home-grown peaches to take home, so I shared the peaches around. Everybody was grateful, but then the fella turned to me and said, 'There's a grub in this peach.' I looked at him and said, 'I know. That's why I gave it to you!' I was just as cheeky as he was. Anyway, that started us talking. It was four hours before we got to South Grafton. South Grafton was a refreshment stop, so he carried my cases up to the bus, so I could go over to my aunt's place, where I was going to stay till my parents came to get me the next day.

We exchanged addresses and Les, that was his name, asked me if I would write. I thought, 'One more pen friend can't hurt.' I wrote to him first and then he wrote back. And the first letter he wrote, he said he didn't like the name Bessie, but he liked Bess, and he already knew what the last part of my name was gunna be. I remember I said to my sister, 'Look at this cheeky bloke!'

The letters increased to about four a week. Then we met. And he asked me to marry him. That's what happened. We saw each other six hours before we got engaged. Despite a lot of my friends saying it won't last, it did. For 54 years.

We laughed about it in later years, because one of my brothers-in-law wrote and asked Mum for my sister's hand, the other one asked Dad for my other sister's. My husband wrote, but he didn't ask, he told them. He knew what he wanted. I loved Mum's letter back—I saw this

> Our parents taught us the lessons in life. If you had a row—a bit of a spat—with your siblings, if you went and told on them to Mum, she'd say, 'Okay, if they are gunna be nasty and not play with you, you can come here and I'll give you a job to do.' We soon learnt that dobbing and telling tales got you nowhere.

letter later in life and it said, 'I never stopped Bessie doing anything in her life and I'm not going to stop her now.' They must have had faith in my choices as well.

We were never game telling our kids what we did, because we didn't know how to handle it if they went out and did the same thing. We tried to analyse it many times, sitting on the verandah—Why did we risk that with one another? We could never work it out, why we were so certain after just six hours. Neither of us. But we had a great life together. I felt safe with him, I felt safe, like I was with Dad. He had the same sort of values that my father had instilled in us—to love your neighbour and treat others like you'd want to be treated yourself.

∞

When we were kids up Tallawudjah Creek, we had a family living next door. Now, I know the lady had had a stroke, but in those days I didn't. She just sat in a cane chair. Dear old Mrs Haze. And Mum sent me up all the time to play with Mavis, her granddaughter. And every day I'd go with some food—something on a plate with a tea towel tied around it.

When I came back here to live—we came back in 1982 and I'm talking about the 1930s—and Mavis, that little girl that I played with, was living down the end of the street here. I went down to see her after I settled in and she said, 'I'll never forget you and your mother. We would have starved, if not for your mother.' I'd never realised at the time—Mum or Dad sending us with food to do the neighbourly thing. Dad used to say to us, 'Never row with your neighbour, because you never know when you might need them.'

When my husband died, I think I failed the grieving course. In those days you were advised to go to counselling. I went twice, that's it, because the doctor that was doing the course said you had to feel angry. I couldn't come to terms with that. You are responsible for your own actions. When you get up in the morning you choose to be happy or you choose to be sad. They said, 'You've gotta go through this angry thing, you've got to be angry with Les for dying.' I couldn't be angry with him, and therefore I couldn't sit there and be miserable. Why would you do that?

I say to people I'm lonely for him, but I'm not lonely for people. I think if you sit in the house and feel sorry for yourself, no one will want to come and see you. We had about three weeks to nut it out, and he came to terms with it and so did I. No regrets … I suppose if I had any regrets it would be education, but life is an education.

TWO PEAS IN A POD

Ann and Lindsay leaving the church after their wedding. (See page 76.)

AUB FROM TENTERFIELD

BORN IN MACLEAN, 1920

I'd been in Tenterfield for about a week and there was a dance on, and these fellas from Bourke asked me, 'Hey Aub, do you dance?' Before I could say anything this other fella says, 'Does he dance! Have you heard of Fred Astaire? Well, Aub's related to him. Aub taught *him* how to dance.'

Anyhow, an old fella, a stockman, Mick Jordon was his name, said, 'I'd like to have a couple of beers with you first.' So I said, 'Right-oh.' So we went to the Tele'. We always drank there. As young fellas in those early days we'd be in there every evening—Oh, we had the time of our bloody lives!

Anyhow, by then the first dance was over and all the Bourke fellas come up here to have a beer. The women weren't allowed to go into the bars in those days, so they'd go into the lounge room. Anyhow, those fellas were saying, 'That bloody Aub, he's all talk, isn't he? He's not dancing.'

So I finished my beer with Mick and headed to the dance. And I said to the fellas, 'I suppose I won't get much of a dance here tonight, because I'm new in town.' So, anyhows, we goes into the dance hall and they all got up dancing. And these two girls were sittin' there, see. That's Noreen—she was sittin' there. I thought, 'Oh, geez. She's a good sort!'

So I asked her for a dance and she said, 'I can't dance much.' Then she said, 'You're not from here, are you?' She was only 17. I said, 'How did you know?' She said, 'It's a small town!' Anyhow, she said she was learning to dance and I said so am I. But see, I could do a bloody gypsy tap on my head!

So we started dancing and she said, 'By geez, you're going all right!' Bit of a liar, wasn't I? Anyway, we finished the dance, then I picked up her friend and had a dance with her, then I got around with them all. I was having a ball, I was, with all these young sheilas. Then it come time for the supper waltz.

Dancing is my passion; I started dancing when I was very young. I was walking girls home from the dance when I was 13. When I'd finish a dance I'd let out a bit of a 'Cooeee!' Oh yeah, I was a good dancer, I love dancing—dancing is how I met my wife.

Aub and Noreen on their wedding day.

They used to go round with a clothes basket full of cups, see. There'd be cooking and sandwiches, they had bloody stuff everywhere. Nor said, 'Right-oh. You can sit with us, that's alright.' Then to make a long story short, it came to the medley. Anyhow, I said, 'Listen love, can I walk you home?' And you know what she said? She said, 'I wouldn't walk across the road with you! They all like dancing with you, but they all reckon you're a cheeky young thing.'

Anyhow, that was okay. Two dances later she did decide I could walk home with her and we were together 68 years after that. The rest is history!

―❧―

Yeah, Nor was a beauty. After a few years she could dance. She could really dance. In the end she was a bloody ripper—she just knew every step of mine. And she had a good heart. I went up to her and said 'Nor'—that's what I used to call her—I said, 'Nor, it's a gypsy tap, are you ready?' She said, 'Look, Aub, those poor little girls over there haven't had a dance all night. Would you go over and have a dance with each one of them, please?' See, Nor, she was never jealous. She liked to share me around with them all. She was a beauty.

Two Peas in a Pod

Kathy: We met at a dance one Saturday night. It was just an ordinary dance. It was about 26 or 27 July, 1954. It was a great night. One of our friends came over and introduced us. Yeah, that was 1954 because last year we forgot the anniversary!
Norm: First time ever we forgot the date. Then we both remembered about the same time, a couple of days later.
Kathy: Well, it's been 60 years since we met. But, yeah, that night, yeah, it was great.

KATHY & NORM
FROM CENTRAL TILBA

KATHY, BORN IN THE
ATHERTON TABLELANDS, 1937
NORM, BORN IN COBARGO, 1932

Norm: The dances up north in those days were incredible. White shirts, shiny shoes and ties for the blokes; and the women were all fancy.

GWENETH & BRIAN
FROM PERTH

GWENETH, BORN IN PERTH, 1928
BRIAN, BORN IN PERTH, 1923

GWENETH: We first met when I was training [during World War II], and I was off duty. I always used to go to Anzac House, because there was always a dance on Saturday nights for girls and boys to all meet up.

This one night we all went to a dance—all us girls, sitting against the wall like wall flowers, waiting for the men to choose. Anyway, Brian came across the floor and asked me for a dance, but he was staggering. I said, 'No, I'm not dancing with you. You're drunk!'

BRIAN: I wasn't drunk ... I'd just had a few refreshments and the floor was a bit slippery.

Gweneth: So he said, 'All right.' Then he asked a friend of mine next to me to dance. And he ended up going with her for three years.

Well, that was that. I didn't see him for a few years and I went to Queensland.

BRIAN: It just so happened that I was leasing a farm adjacent to Gwen's sister.

GWENETH: I came back [to Western Australia] to help on my sister's farm because she had kids, close together, and she was finding it a bit hard to look after everyone. So I went to help out.

Anyway, I had a female dog and it kept running away. It kept going over to the neighbour's property and coming back with another dog.

BRIAN: Her female dog kept enticing my dog to run away. You know, you can't tell animals what to do. The only way is to lock 'em up, but you can't do that. So I had to go get the dog from her sister's place and 12 months later I was engaged. That's what happened. I went to get my dog and I got trapped, myself. Caught by the foot!

GWENETH: He didn't fight very hard to get away!

BRIAN: Hmmm.

GWENETH: Yes, after 12 months we were engaged. At Christmas time. And then married in April.

BRIAN: And 61 years later, she's still got me by the leg and tells me what to do.

GWENETH: Oh, please!

Brian: One of the reasons I think we've gotten on so well is because I've got a very good understanding of Gwen's background. I know where she grew up, I know where she came from. I knew her family and I respected them.

> I haven't been to the city for 45 or 46 years. I'd hate to go back now. I see enough on TV with them bloody traffic jams. Geez, it must be boring driving in the city, just sitting there. I ride my horses into town.

LES 'ROOSTER'
FROM HILL END

BORN IN MUDGEE, 1931

I met my wife at Hargraves Dance Hall. I remember that night, she had a blue dress on. They said, 'Select your partners for a barn dance.' So I went over and asked Joan for a dance. Anyhow, we danced round and got a bit friendly and that's how it all started—we were married 48 years. She's passed on now; she had heart problems and the heart ended up getting her. She was 72. She's buried just up here at the cemetery.

BONNIE
FROM WALLAGOOT
BORN IN SYDNEY, 1922

Growing up, my mum meant everything to me. But I lost her just after my ninth birthday; she was only 49. She used to play the violin—that's where my love of music came from—and she used to paint. She really was a lovely lady. A very kind lady. I've got a lot of lovely memories of my mum. My father, on the other hand, was a seafaring man, so I didn't see much of him; there was not a lot of contact at all. After Mum passed, I was lucky to have an older sister that took over my upbringing. I was very lucky to have her. She was newly married when Mum died, so I was lucky her husband didn't object to me being there.

My sister moved around a lot and we ended up in Beverly Hills, near Hurstville, for a while. Then we moved to Coogee—we were in a semi-detached house there. The family that lived next door to us—there was a boy and a girl—the boy was my age. We were the worst enemies, but the best friends. He was an absolute larrikin. That didn't worry me because we were real good mates. We used to go to the movies and everything together. We did so much. He was my best friend. But that's another story …

I got my first job when I was 14. I got 13s 6d a week. It was at a milliners' shop in Her Majesty's Arcade in Sydney. She was a lovely lady who owned the shop—Miss Sutherland. Then I got a job as a telephonist, but the hours were a bit much. My sister wanted to move on, so we moved to a poultry farm for a while and I worked there. Then I worked in a handbag shop. When we moved again, to Greenacre, I got a job at the Metro Theatre—the drive-in theatre. I was there for 23 years. I was there four months after it opened, until it closed. Woolworths are there now. Woolworths are everywhere!

Anyway, there was a man who worked at the theatre. He managed a little area with the tray boys. He was also an accountant and he helped out with accounts. Over time I learnt a bit about him and he learnt a bit about me. He had two kids. They'd come from Hungary to England to Australia during the war [World War II]. It was a funny sort of friendship that went on and on.

Anyway, I felt sorry for his kids. They weren't little children, but still children. The talk of marriage didn't come up for a long time. We got engaged, but I broke it, I just couldn't seem to bring myself to settle down with somebody. Anyway, a few more years went by and in the long run we did get married.

Anyway, Jim got cancer. I did all I could for him, but it was never enough. I never seemed to do the right thing. He was 69 when he passed away.

I suppose I should tell you about the tragedy during the war. This young fella that had lived next to us—the one I told you about—he was conscripted into the army. He didn't like the army so he joined the air force. His name was Tom, but he was known as Chappy to everybody. He was an absolute larrikin. I have so many memories of Chappy. Whenever my sister would take me out to town he would come, too. Anyway, one day, we were in a furniture shop and Chappy had a banana with him. We ate the banana together—I can still see him do it, he was only a kid—and he put the skin in one of the drawers of a dressing table and left it there. We went back to that store months later and the banana skin was still in that drawer. It was stuck to the wood. He was so cheeky at times.

He could also upset me at times, too. I remember one time, he got really mad and grabbed all my Nelson Eddy scrapbooks—I loved Nelson Eddy music—and he threw them up on the roof. That really upset me. In the long run he went and got them back. I don't know what it was, but he knew how to push my buttons.

When he went away, Chappy wrote me many times. He wrote about the theatres overseas and said how much I would have enjoyed them. In one of the letters

It was a terrible thing. Had he come home—there was nothing definite— but had he come home, I think ... Unfortunately, it was just one of those things, and it happened to be him. So many of them got killed.

Bonnie and Chappy before he left for the war.

he wrote me he said, 'What I'd give now to be sitting in the lounge room, listening to Nelson Eddy ...'

We got the first telegram. We were sitting at the table. It was a Sunday dinner. And the boy came on the bike with a little brown envelope. That was the start of it—to say Chappy was missing. He was a pilot in a bomber. The telegrams went on for some time. Then we got the news—he had been killed. We were all around the table ... it was an awful day. I cried and I cried and I cried.

The sad part about it was, everything he liked, I liked. He loved music, I liked music. He liked the theatre, so did I. It just seemed such a shame. I've still got all the telegrams when he was missing. And then the last one ... I've kept his letters. My niece, Julie, knows they've got to go in the box with me when I go.

You know the saddest part? Apparently, you had to fly 32 trips before you got a break and then you could come home on leave. And what happens—his bomber was shot down on the thirty-second flight. His last trip. His last trip before he would have come home.

He was the one and only. I tried to make the best of my marriage, but it was hard. I always thought about Chappy ... It's too late now, but all my life, I've wondered, if only—what might have been.

Brian and Beryl on their wedding day in 1952.

BERYL & BRIAN
FROM HAHNDORF

BERYL, BORN HAHNDORF, 1932
BRIAN, BORN IN MT BARKER, 1930

BERYL: Brian came up here when he was 14 and he had a job at Smith's Bakery, in Hahndorf, in the shop. I didn't know him then.

BRIAN: In Year 7 I got a scholarship to go to the Adelaide High School, but my mother needed me to bring in an income, so at 14 I had to pack up and find a job. I came back to Hahndorf, coincidently, because the baker down here was friends with my mother. A bit more than friends! So he arranged for me to come and work there. I lived in there and he was paying me 25s a week plus keep.

I used to help deliver the bread around town on the horse and cart. I remember one time, one weekend, we had to get another horse for the cart— one was crook. So the baker drove me to Adelaide and I rode the horse up the old road back to Hahndorf. I'd never ridden a horse before that, and I've never ridden one since!

BERYL: I was allowed to go to the dances when I was 14 or 15. I used to go with my brother. I must admit I had a couple of beaut fellas who used to dance with me, but I never went out with any of them. I remember one of them asked me if he could walk me home one night and I said, 'No, I'm too young to go out with boys.'

There were a couple of boys I had my eye on, but I just knew when I met Brian that I wanted to marry him and that was it. And we did.

Two Peas in a Pod 73

Brian: I think the main lesson you can learn in life is to have good family support. That didn't come from my side, that came from her side. Her side had a very strong family. If I've learnt anything in my time, it's marry the right woman. We've been a good team through good times and bad.
Beryl: Yes, we've been a good team and we still are.

Brian: I learnt to dance at Beryl's place in the dining room.
Beryl: That's right. We all used to learn to dance up in our home. Dad had an old gramophone and we all learnt to dance and waltz in the dining room. He'd move the table out and roll up the carpet and we'd all dance to the music. I believe that's how a lot of people learnt to dance, in their own homes. Down at Granny's we would play the piano and dance. I tell you, it was such a happy, lovely time.

My father thought the world of Brian. And so did my mother. My mother eventually had to go into care, into the nursing home. My sister and I couldn't manage her anymore. Well, Brian would just pick her up in his arms, carry her, put her in the back of the car and bring her home for the day. He was always very gentle with older people.

We married in the Anglican church on 15 November 1952. My granny died that year, in August, which was sad. She was only 72. But it was lovely—my baby sister was three and a half, and my other sister was there. And my friend Norma from over the road was my bridesmaid. And Brian had his brother and friend Ross as groomsmen at the wedding.

We had two children. Our son grew up and went to Sydney and did a Bachelor's [degree] in Physiology. He wanted to do his Masters, but he died in 1989. You have to move on after something like that, and Brian was my strength. Our daughter worked at Westpac Bank and she loved her work. She married and had a son in 1992. But she died a few years ago, in 2009—she had a bad stroke at 52. So we've had two children and then lost them, but we've still got each other.

ANN AND LINDSAY
FROM OLD BAR

ANN, BORN IN NEWCASTLE, 1949
LINDSAY, BORN IN TAREE, 1937

ANNE: When we were growing up I didn't know him, but he knew me because he was 12 years older than me. He used to bring the cart around.

LINDSAY: I used to drive a horse and cart around Old Bar—I used to rear pigs up on the old farm. And all the mothers around the place used to keep their food scraps for me, for the pigs. I used to come around with this spring cart, with three 44-gallon drums on it. Anne's sister used to jump on the cart and get a ride down the road every time I come past. But Anne was a bit shyer than Penny.

> Lindsay: All the ladies around the place used to keep their scraps for me—they were all chasing me for their daughters.

Two Peas in a Pod

I no forget him.
I no forget.

I come from Croatia with two boys, my husband and me. I come to Sydney, then 11 days Bonegilla [migrant camp], Victoria. After, we go to Whyalla. After we get a house, my husband work BHP. I have a daughter, then she two months old I come to Adelaide. Then come here. My husband, I, very happy here, Australia.

ANDJA
FROM COOBER PEDY

BORN IN CROATIA, DATE UNKNOWN

My husband passed away 8 May 2006, at 11 o'clock in the morning. The day before, [TV journalist] Richard Carlton passed away, Tasmania. He said to me, 'Andja, come here.' He no understand news Richard Carlton. I say, 'What are you talking? You come same Australia like myself. Why I need to tell you what TV said?' He said, 'Andja, my head empty, I no English this morning, I dunno English this morning, none.' I sit down next to him, here. He put his head down my shoulder. Right shoulder. From his eye, tear. He passed away, my shoulder. I no forget him.

FRED & ISOBEL
FROM BAMBAROO

QLD · 4850

FRED BORN IN INGHAM, 1933
ISOBEL BORN IN INGHAM, 1933

Fred: I've been here 81 years.
Isobel: And I've been here 61 years.
Fred: I'm nine days older than her. I was coming out of the hospital when she was coming in.
Isobel: Yeah, he gave me a wink, back then.
Fred: We met on a train. I had a broken leg and I was with my aunty going to Tully to watch football, and she was going up to play basketball. That was the first time I saw her, but then I met her at a dance.

Fred: After the dance I asked if I could take her home and she said yes. I was so happy, but then I had to walk a bloody mile, back to my motorbike.

Two Peas in a Pod 81

KAY FROM MELBOURNE

BORN IN MELBOURNE, 1929

VIC · 3000

Kay in her TAA uniform.

I remember coming back from the Alfred Hospital on a tram after having my tonsils out. I would have been about four then. I was very upset because I was promised an ice cream, and when I got the ice cream I couldn't swallow it because my throat was too sore, so they gave it to my little brother. I went through all the pain but I didn't get the ice cream. That's my earliest memory.

I was born with a twisted foot. So the doctors put me to toe dancing. I was not a very good toe dancer, but I was a good acrobat. That led to me being in a lot of pantomimes. All my school holidays for the next 12 years was spent on the stage in one of those pantomimes—Princes Theatre, a lot of the main theatres. That then led to me being in the circus. I was about 7 when I was part of the circus. I remember I used to get on the tram and go by myself. I travelled around quite a lot as a child. You weren't scared in those days. Or perhaps my mother didn't care too much about me.

After the Depression my mother was living alone with two small children. My mother was on her own and I think it was difficult. I remember I had whooping cough very badly and I was still sent to dancing school with whooping cough. I coughed all over the place. My dancing teacher, who knew a doctor, asked the doctor, 'Can you do something with this child?' The doctor said, 'Not unless I take her home.'

My mother agreed to this, she said, 'Yes, that's all right.' I suppose it was good to get one kid off her plate. So he took me home and he and his wife and his sister-in-law took care of me. I was there until I was 10 or 11. And my brother was sent to … like, homes. Children's homes. He was always being sent somewhere, because my mother had to work. It was difficult in those days.

I don't know what she did. I wasn't with her in those days. But she came to take me back. And she had rooms. Apartment rooms. She would rent a large place and then

Kay as a young girl with her mother.

rent the rooms out. That was about all she could do. She did that right up until she died. My grandpa, who was a magistrate, they didn't get on too well. I don't know what happened. He would come and see me, but didn't get on with her. I think she disappointed him in some way.

I was quite lucky because I got looked after where I stayed. But my brother wasn't so lucky. He was shifted around a lot. He died when he was 45. I miss him a lot.

I never knew anything about my father. I never found out anything about him. My mother used to say she changed her mind a bit. She told me he walked into the sea at one stage. So I never knew anything about him. My aunt told me he was English, but that's all I ever knew. She said he used to call me his 'little English rose'. There must have been someone, somewhere. I always wondered where he was and what happened to him. That was a bit sad.

I went to school, when I stayed with the doctor. I went to a little school that only went to Third Grade. I used to come home with ribbons, like a cow. Anyway, he was a very flamboyant kind of person. He used to sit at a grand piano in a red velvet jacket. He had a lot of ladies who were very interested in him and he gave quite lavish parties. And because I was a dancer, he would bring me out and make me perform for everyone. Like a seal. He'd say, 'Come and perform, darling.'

Then he would say to his sister-in-law, 'Take it away. Put it to bed.' He was very kind, but he was not very interested in children. He went to China and I didn't see him again until I was about 18.

Aunty Dot, who was the sister-in-law, who really looked after me, she was the most stable thing in my life. After the doctor left I went to live with her, in several different places. People didn't have houses in those days, they rented. She didn't have much money, but she took good care of me. All these people looked after me, but none of them were related to me.

⁂

When I left school I wanted to be a pharmacist. In those days you had to be an apprentice to a pharmacist and you had to pay to do that. I worked in a pharmacy at Flinders Street Station. I've got pictures of that. I went to work there and the pharmacist said he would teach me for free, but because I lived in a small flat and only got a small wage, I couldn't afford to do that. I always regret that.

I left and went into theatre. I married a musician. I was only 21. I think I did that to show my mother I could get away from her. It was a silly thing to do, really. It just didn't work out. He was a party person. And I wasn't. I worked at the State Theatre, and the Palais in St Kilda for a while. Then I met a girlfriend who wanted to be an air hostess. She asked me if I would come and do the first aid course with her. Then she said, 'Why don't you come and apply?' I said, 'It's not my thing, but just for the hell of it, I'll apply.' Well, she didn't make it, but I did. I don't think I saw much of her after that. It was a turn in my life that I didn't expect.

Working for TAA [Trans Australia Airlines] meant you had to go along and ask every person if they had flown before, because most people hadn't. Then you had to explain to every person the procedures. Then you would go along and offer magazines. Then you would offer barley sugar. That was all before you took off. Then, when you were in the air, you had to go along with urns and you might have steak and onion in one urn and mash potato in another. You had to go along and dish out to everyone. On your own. That was commercial flying in 1954 and 1955, but I had to leave that job because I was getting married again.

Unfortunately, that marriage didn't work out the way I'd hoped either and soon enough I found myself with two children and no money. He'd been the son of an entrepreneur, and he'd never really had to do anything else. When I came to Melbourne he was living in a Toorak mansion, driving a Jaguar and everything. Everything seemed to be lovely at first, but his dad was the one who held them together. But, unfortunately, when his dad died, things fell apart. My husband liked to play golf, but he didn't want to do anything. He just wasn't trained to do anything. He didn't bother paying bills. So, when his father died, consequently, we lost the house, we lost everything.

He wasn't a bad person, he just couldn't cope. He didn't know what to do with his life. I couldn't stand the fact that we had bailiffs coming through the house. I couldn't bear it; I didn't care, just so long as I didn't owe any money to anyone. So I left.

So, I ended up back at my mother's, renting a single bedroom with a share bathroom and kitchen, with my two children, for three years. Linda was three and John was five. I had to pay £5 10s a week. My mum charged me exactly the same as what she charged other guests. Not a penny less. It was hard to go back to that.

Their father used to come and take the kids on the weekend, but then he got a melanoma and he died very quickly. Within a few months. I wanted to help him in the end but I couldn't afford to. So his brother looked after him.

One night, a friend, Bill, invited me to a square dance. I wasn't a very good dancer, but Bill was very kind to me and always wanted to help. Anyway, he asked one night, 'Would you like to come to a square dance?' I don't know why, because I wasn't good at all, but for some reason I said, 'Yes, I'll go.'

He was picking me up in a car. He was also picking up a friend, a guy who had been a rocket scientist working in Scotland and Ireland for a year, for the government. This friend, Barrie, had just come home for Christmas and was flying back to England for 12 months. Apparently he'd sold his car, so Bill had to pick him up, and me up. So the two of us rode in the car together. Barrie was quite nice and polite, and everything.

Anyway, we danced that night. He did a lot of improvising, and he was tying me up in knots, because I couldn't do it, and he was laughing and laughing. I thought he was such a nice person. He's lovely. The rest of the dancers weren't so happy with me, but he was laughing and we had a good time. I thought, 'What a shame he's leaving, he's such a nice person.'

Anyway, Bill drove us home and dropped me off and I asked Bill, 'Do you think Barrie would write me as a pen friend? I'd love to hear what he's doing over there.'

Anyway, Barrie was kind enough to write to me. We wrote for a while, but I thought, 'I won't keep doing this, he's this rocket scientist working for the government in foreign countries, and here I am living in this little room with my two children. He wouldn't be interested in me.' I thought it was silly. But I kept writing because I thought, 'I won't see him, so it doesn't matter.'

But then he was away 12 months and then he came back. He rang through and said, 'I'm here, I'm back. Would you like to go out?' It was hard to say no, but I was thinking, 'He's going to come to this place and see how I live.'

My mother was delighted having me stay at her place, because I was under her thumb again. She didn't want any intruders coming into my life that might take me away. So what she did was ... I had said to the children, who were still quite little, I said, 'Nanna's going to put you to bed, and I'll be back soon.' So I gave them a kiss and said goodbye. The place had a very long path down to the sidewalk where Barrie was waiting ...

Now, in all the letters I'd written to Barrie, I'd never mentioned the children, because I thought, 'He's just a pen friend.' So he didn't know. He knew I'd been married, but didn't know I had children. So I came down the path and as I got close and smiled, my mother let the children go; she could have held them back but she wanted to spoil the moment. They ran down, 'Mummy, mummy!' He didn't bat an eyelid. He greeted me and the children as though he had known all along.

We went out several times and I thought, 'This is really hard on him meeting someone with children.' I knew it wasn't going to go any further than that. But it was nice going out with him a few times. At one stage I said to him, 'I'll go out with you till Christmas, but then you've got to find a nice girl with no attachments.' I thought, 'He shouldn't take on the responsibility of us, he was too nice a person.'

He wouldn't have that, and eventually the place next door to my mother's came up for sale. He went to the auction and was the only person there. He knocked the price down and bought it. He turned it into flats.

He was living with his parents, working as a scientist during the day and coming down and stripping wallpaper at night. Fixing the place up. Anyway, he said 'Move the children into one of these flats on the side.' The children didn't know he owned it. I'd told them that someone had let us use it.

At first I'd just go in and cook dinner and bath the children, and then I'd get them back next door before he came down. So they didn't see him. He was coming in the front door as we were going out the back. Then after a while he convinced me to move in. My mother wasn't happy about that, because then she didn't have control anymore.

My son, John, was absolutely ecstatic. He wrote this note about all the things that were going to be good about moving into this flat and having more space—

Barrie: Things are vague in my memory now, but that evening when the kids ran out, it didn't worry me. When I was in England, Kay had sent me a picture of herself—there was her shadow and then there was a another smaller shadow, so I'd had an inkling.

being able to have friends over, not having to climb under the bed to put the power on and all those sort of things. It wasn't anything amazing, it was one bedroom and a lounge room, but we had our own kitchen and our own bathroom. Linda doesn't remember much about it, but John was ecstatic.

We moved in permanently then, but they still didn't see him, because they were completely separate flats. We had our own entrance. But we were so grateful that someone was looking after us. Eventually it was the children who actually ended up proposing to him. They said, 'Will you marry our mother?'

It gave us a different life, right up until this very day. Barrie has been marvellous to the children. After a year I thought, 'Barrie deserved a child of his own,' although I don't think he would have minded if he didn't, and that's why I had the third child. He said he didn't mind, but I think he was very pleased.

So that's the story up till now. We married in 1965 and have been together ever since.

Daph in her Australian Women's Army uniform. (See page 92.)

ONE & THREEPENCE A WEEK

BOB
FROM HILL END
BORN IN SYDNEY, 1937

NSW · 2850

My father introduced me to a cross-cut saw when I was about 10 or 11. He seemed to have arms that were about six feet long. I spent more time running forwards and backwards trying to keep up with the handle than I did helping him cut. I haven't got any fond memories of that cross-cut saw.

When I turned 15 in March, I got myself a job on a sheep property, because there was a lot of wool-growing going on around here back then. My first week's wage was £2 17s 2d. You worked five and a half days a week. I worked there for a couple of years, then started cutting trees for a crust. I used to like the little three and a half pound axe. It was similar to the four pounder, but it was a bit thinner. It was magic for cutting green timber.

> We always had chores. We had to get a barrow-load of wood every night to keep the fire going. So of a weekend you'd take the horse and sled out to collect wood.

ARCHIE
FROM TI TREE
BORN IN NAPPERBY, DATE UNKNOWN

When I was a young man, big army travels through. Lots of men. Going through to Darwin [during World War II]. No schooling, I was working—working all my life—20 years working at the school for Mr Kin. Yeah. Long time mowing grass. Yeah. I working horses too, long days on horseback, driving cattle across country, all the way to Queensland. Then we riding horses back. Long time riding. We take camels. Carry water and tucker. I been working for long time, always working. When I not working I sit down.

COL
FROM AIRLY
BORN IN MUDGEE, 1937

NSW · 2846

I found the first diamond in 1961. I had trouble convincing geologists it was a diamond—until I started to sell a few of them. But I got support from the local miners. A baggy-arsed bloke like me, just out of the army, no dollars. They all helped me. My coal mine boss in Lithgow, Basil—rest in peace Basil—sold me a broken-down bulldozer for 75 quid. I tugged it home and rebuilt the thing and started to cut this road up the mountain.

Anyway, the years went by ... In 1975 I worked at the local coal mine and all the time, in my spare time, I was working putting together a washing plant on this property. Then gold prices started to sky rocket from 30 quid an ounce, it went up to a 100 quid an ounce. I thought, 'That's interesting,' because there was a lot of gold up there. So I said to the wife, 'I've never borrowed money for the mine before, but I'm gunna borrow $5000.' She said, 'Go ahead, you've been a good provider.' Five thousand dollars was equivalent to two Corollas back then. So I borrowed and I finished the plant off. And within six days I had mined gold and diamonds and other gems worth over $5800.

Then to jump ahead a bit, the blokes I was selling the diamonds to offered me $300,000 for a per cent of the mine. So we shared it amongst ourselves. That's about a million bucks in today's terms.

But mining can be dangerous work. The thing was you used to have to go in under the old basalt and dig under the old river. Some of them are so fresh it's just digging sand out with your hands. I was always up there on my lonesome. And one spot there, I was digging a trench in real soft white sand. I'd dug in about 12 foot, up to about shoulder depth. I was working down on my hands and knees under about four foot of sand. I stopped and backed out to about knee level to clear my pockets and roll a smoke. I hardly got my tobacco out of my pocket and WHOMP, the whole lot fell in. Just like water. It just flopped in, without a sound. I was standing there in a foot of sand and I couldn't pull my legs out. I had to dig 'em out, it was so tight. That got my heart going, when I realised how close I'd come to being buried alive. I climbed the ladder and had a smoke and had a talk to God. I said, 'Thanks mate.'

Boy, it was good being rich! I was able to give my kids their will money and watch them spend it. It was more fun watching 'em spend it than it was spending it myself.

DAPH
FROM WALLABADAH

BORN IN BARRABA, 1924

I left Barraba when I was 11 years old and we went to Newcastle to live. I went to Warners Bay Public for my last year of primary school and then to Newcastle Girls' High School. I was 16 and a half when I finished my exams and then I had a job in an office. Shorthand and typing and all that sort of thing. I was coming out of that office in February 1942 and there was a big kerfuffle in the streets. The paper boys were yelling out, 'Darwin bombed! Darwin bombed!'

I thought, 'That's it, I'll be 18 in June, I'm going to join one of the services.' So that's what I did. I went into the Women's Army in 1942, just after my birthday. I went down on a troop train to Sydney and signed all the papers. Got all the needles and all that. And got sent to Randwick for rookies' training. All the marching and rules and all that sort of thing.

There were 100 of us girls. They nominated where we were to go. Well, I got sent back to Newcastle because they reckoned I'd be good on the anti-aircraft batteries.

So 26 of us got put on a troop train to Newcastle. The only women amongst a whole trainload of men. At Newcastle station the men got picked up and disappeared and there was just us girls left on the platform. Our sergeant, who'd been selected before we left, went up to a couple of soldiers who were standing on the platform. And she went up and she said, 'Are you here to get the reinforcements for the anti-aircraft batteries?' And this male sergeant said, 'Yes. Why?' She said, 'Well, that's us!' And he said, 'But you're bloody women! What am I gunna do with women?' He hadn't seen women in the army before. We hadn't either! Some of us didn't even have a proper uniform because there hadn't been enough manufactured at that stage.

Anyway, we got split into two groups. Fourteen went on to an anti-aircraft battery and 12 of us went to an air force base to do secret work in the operations room. It was a converted school, and it was where all the information came in and where the air force plotted the air force, the navy and the army. We looked down on the plotting area.

It was all top secret, of course, and the first time I went home on leave, my father, who didn't want me to go in the army, said, 'Right-oh. What are you doing?' I said, 'I'm a cook.' He said, 'Don't be stupid, you can't even boil water!' We were told not to tell our parents anything about what we did. So I said, 'Sorry Pop, I can't tell you. I'm doing secret work.' He was happy then. He never knew for years what I was actually doing.

Eventually, I became a computer operator. Not like today's computers, there was no such thing. But us women could do it quicker than the men. We would get a phone message of where a plane was leaving—what plane it was and what base it was leaving—and we had to work all these rulers and things and measure the wind and the height it would be flying and all that. And estimate

what time it would be over Newcastle so the people on the anti-aircraft batteries would know this is a DC3, so they'd know not to put any alarm on or anything.

Things were pretty grim in 1942 after Newcastle had been shelled. We didn't know if the Japs were going to come or not. After we'd been there for 10 months we had to switch over with the girls who'd been out on the battery—so the 'Powers That Be' experimented with us to confirm that we could do all that the men did.

So 1942 was a stressful time, but it was also a wonderful time. I was engaged to be married. My soldier boy had proposed to me just before I went into the army. He went off to Darwin when all the air raids went on there. And stayed there until February 1944.

We decided to get married in forty-four, but I didn't have as much leave saved up as he did. I applied for compassionate leave, but they wouldn't give it to me.

So I went AWOL. We got married and went on our honeymoon to Katoomba—Katoomba was the place for honeymoons! The military police went out to my mother's place and wanted to know where I was. Anyhow, when I got back I got arrested, of course. And I lost my stripes.

After they decided that there was no more danger of being bombed by Japs, they disbanded anti-aircraft and all of us got sent to different postings. I got put into coastal artillery as a plotter and a gunner. We had to learn all about shipping. But that was alright. In fact, at one of the places I had more fun than any other. We were at a radar station where we had to identify all the ships. We had all these big telescopes and things.

Most people accepted us, our role in the army. The idea of all the Women's Services was so we could take on the men's work and the men could go to New Guinea,

> Apart from losing [my husband] Sid and Mum early, I've been fortunate. I've been lucky, yeah, things are pretty good. I've got lovely neighbours. I've got a wonderful family and friends. Yeah, if I fall off the perch tomorrow, I'll say I've enjoyed my life.

Daph with her husband, Sid, returning to service after their honeymoon.

and because it was so desperate there the Japs looked like getting here. The ones that didn't want to go to New Guinea, they didn't like us. But the majority of fellas were quite happy to go and serve.

After the war ended we lived with my mum and dad and then we bought five acres of land next door. My brother-in-law, my father and my husband built us a little house. We stayed there until we moved to Wallabadah in 1950. My husband hated Newcastle. He was a real bushy. We only stayed in Newcastle because my mother had cancer. She died in 1948.

In 1966 we bought a little farm of our own. We had a little war service house built on it. Unfortunately in 1984 Sid passed away. One afternoon, he went down to his garden, which was 50 metres from the house. He said, 'I'll be up at four o'clock.' We used to have a game of darts every afternoon and have a beer. And he said, 'I'll be up at four o'clock and I'm gunna beat you today.' Because I must have beat him the day before, which was something rare, because he was the best dart player. Anyway, four o'clock came and he hadn't arrived.

He was a very punctual person so I looked down in the garden and I couldn't see him. But one of the doors on the shed was open, so I thought he must be in the shed. And with that his dog came up. I said, 'What are you doing here, Toby? Go back to Dad.' The dog turned around and off he went. A few minutes later Toby was back again at the kitchen door. I looked at the clock and by then it was ten past four, and I got a funny feeling, and I looked down and I couldn't see him in the garden and the shed was still open. So I went down. And he'd passed away. In the garden. It was a big shock, he'd had a massive heart attack. I tried to revive him, because I'd had first-aid training. But I knew he was gone.

I went straight from school to *The Age* office—in the circulation department. I used to go around with the inspectors in their cars—around to the various agents and see what their grizzles were. I stayed at the paper for a while, then I joined the army. When I came back from the army, I went back to the newspaper for a short time. Then I did some study, then I went into the Postmaster-General's Office as a telephone technician. From there I went to army design—into the armament section. I left army design and went to Aeronautical Research Laboratory (ARL). I stayed there till I retired.

I played a bit of footy when I was young. Started off at Sandringham in the VFA [Victorian Football Association], and from there went to North Melbourne in forty-seven. I played a handful of senior games there. Then I got an approach from Moorabbin to go and play for them in the VFA. Played a couple of seasons. Later on I coached them. We got a premiership at Moorabbin. After that, St Kilda came down and grabbed the ground and that put Moorabbin out of the VFA. So from there I went up to Prahran, in the VFA. We won a premiership up there, too.

GRAHAM
FROM MELBOURNE

BORN IN MELBOURNE, 1924

VIC · 3000

I coached Kevin Sheedy for three years at Prahran. He was a peculiar bloke. He grew up in Prahran in the slums but he had such a great ability to pull himself up. He's made a name for himself all over Australia—from a kid who grew up in Prahran.

JOHN
FROM BRISBANE
BORN IN GREECE, 1932

I immigrated to Australia from Greece on a ship in 1952. We ended up at an immigration camp in Bonegilla in Victoria, waiting for the government to find us a job. They found me a job at Port Kembla in Wollongong. So I went there and worked [at the refinery] for about six months. But I found it was dangerous, unhealthy work. They never gave us masks and you could see the iron run down your face like a big creek. I thought that wasn't a very healthy place, so I left.

Then I got a job at the Capitol Café in Wollongong ... then I cut sugar cane for six years. I worked in mines as a fitter and turner. I picked grapes in Mildura; I picked peas in Port Pirie; pears in Sheparton, Leeton, Riverton, Griffith, Narrandera ... Ahhh, I had a big café in Broken Hill, with a couple of partners.

Then I left and went to work in Papua New Guinea in 1963, for nearly 20 years. I was building roads in Papua, shooting crocodiles. I've been declared the most capable of crocodile taxidermists. I'm a self-taught taxidermist. I love to do the crocodile taxidermy. I'm the original crocodile man, back in the sixties. Oh yeah, man, they could make a movie about me.

I got another job, then another. I can't count my jobs, I had a hell of a lot of jobs— about 50 different kinds of work. No one has had as many jobs as me.

After school I got a job working on the farm Dad was working on. I was 15. Dad was managing the property, I was pumping water, carting wood with the horse and cart to the marble quarry—cutting it up with an axe, in big lengths so he could feed it into the bloody boiler. That was one of the first jobs that I did. 'General farm work', you'd call it. We worked hard. And we worked long hours, too. We worked from daylight till dark.

The general farm work continued on, with the drenching of sheep, the catching of bloody rabbits and the growing of crops. Up until I started driving the horse team, where I yoked 10 horses up, then done the ploughing and worked the ground down, and put the horses onto the combine and sowed the grain or wheat or whatever we were sowing. And when the crop grew, the binder come into the situation. The sheaf hay, right, tied into round sleeves, about seven pound weight to each sheaf. It was left to dry out for about eight to 10 days, then it was loaded onto the horse wagons with a pitchfork, one sheaf at a time, and then stacked in the hay shed.

A little bit before 1950 the boss that owned the property at that time, he up and died. At 68. He had a stroke and died. He had two sons. So they took over the property.

So, anyway, this younger boss, Keith Hockey was his name, said to Dad, 'I think you better get rid of the horses and I'll bring

MERVIN
FROM TARANA

BORN IN BATHURST, 1927

NSW • 2787

> I never spent a bloody razoo. Me mum and dad kept me, in other words. Thanks to them what money I had, I gradually built up. The first money I spent was when I bought the first model Holden car. And I paid for it in cash money that I'd saved up over the years with the rabbit skins, see. That was the first money that I ever spent.

a tractor down.' The name of the old tractor was Lanz Bulldog. That was the first tractor that I drove, right. To start it up, you have a blow lamp, underneath the front of it to heat it up. Rock it to and fro with the compression. 'Boom, boom, boom,' away she'd go. Single cylinder it was. So, anyway, we had that for a start.

The property was still smothered in a lot of bloody timber, you know. Dry timber. This young boss said to Dad, 'Well, this is no good, we're gunna have to buy a bulldozer,' see. So, anyway, he bought a smaller type bulldozer, not a big one, about the size equal to a D4, you know. So, anyway, he brought it down. He bought it brand new, he brought it down from the west, on a truck. He set me up on it and I cleared all of the property. One paddock at a time, for years. You know, that went on for bloody years.

Anyway, all that time when I was working, in the winter months the rabbits was getting caught. The bloody rabbits were getting caught by the thousands. And rabbit skin money was coming in every month.

Your rabbit skin money varied—depending on the skin buyer and what sort of mood he was in. It was so much a pound if you worked it out and you had good skins—well looked after and so forth. It worked out roughly about 6d a rabbit. Probably for skins it might have been a bit less. When we done some carcass work, the whole rabbit, 1s 1d a pair was the best we got. So you could work it out that each rabbit was worth about 6d, see.

When I started work I got one quid a week. One pound a week. After the old boss had died, I'd been there a few years, then the new fella, the son, after about … I dunno, bloody 12 months, two years, he raised me up to 30 bob a week. He give me 10 bob a week rise. But at the same token he mentioned, 'You might have to do a bit more work,' see. How bloody tough they were!

Of course, that went on a while, wages gradually rose up—a bit now and a bit again—till it got up to £4 2s a week. But we were still catching rabbits at that stage. I was working all week, driving the bloody tractors and doing the farm work, for £4 2s a week. But I trapped the rabbits mainly at night or early morning—making £20 a month out of the bloody rabbits. You could make more money rabbitin' than you could working for wages. You might look at Merv and say, 'He didn't do a whole lot of hard work in his day.' But with a pick and shovel we dug the bloody rabbit burrows out. That was all hard yakka.

Superphosphate, you've heard of that? As the years went on we got all the country cleared. It started to lack a bit, so the superphosphate come into it. The boss ordered super. It came from Port Kembla, on the rail trucks to Newbridge. Me and the other workmen had to cart the super from the railway and stack it in the farm shed. Do you know how much yakka it involved? One hundred tonne! Every year! For a period of about bloody nearly 20 years. You'd pick it up from the rail truck and put it on the motor lorry. When you got home to the

Mum and Dad used to go to Bathurst once every month to get the spare grocery things you couldn't get in the town. Once a month! Today, people want to go to town every bloody second day of the week. That's why you used to make things spin out — because you couldn't afford to be running back and forth, even though petrol was only a song to what it's worth these days.

shed, you picked it up again and stacked it in the shed, right. So, in other words, we picked it up, seven and a half tonne at a time. Picked it up out of the rail truck, put it on the lorry. You took it home to the shed. You picked it up again and put it in the shed. Then to get it out of the shed you picked it up again and put it on the truck and took it out to the paddock. Picked it up again and put it into the super cart. That's four times that you handled 100 bloody tonne. Every year. For 20 years! The bloody sweat would be drippin' off the brow that bloody much it would be wetting the paper bags. You try to get someone to believe that. That's as true as I sit here. You try to get young people to do that today.

   It's a wonder I'm still alive with the amount of yakka I've done in my lifetime. It's only in the last few bloody years that I've sort of fouled up. Me feet and me legs have gone to buggery. When I was young, I could have jumped over the bloody moon.

TED
FROM GUYRA

BORN IN ARMIDALE, 1916

During the Depression years swaggies used to come by the farm all the time, asking for a meal or work. I remember one particular man—he was a wonderful old fellow. He came to our property with a little bit of a swag. My father was a very good-hearted type of person and all this bloke wanted was a bit of food. So, my father said to him, 'Go into the shearers' hut and get yourself something to eat.' Which he did. Then he stopped around for a few days.

There was no work about, so my father said to him, 'I'll give you some rabbit traps. If you go and do a bit of trapping, I'll pay you some scalp money.' This fellow did. And as soon as he got a few bob, this fellow paid everyone back that he owed. He finished up stopping on the farm for four years. He was a wonderful person. He was an old broken-down jockey and to listen to him, he'd tell stories like he'd won a Melbourne cup on a draught horse! His name was Tom and he was just down on his luck.

When war broke out [World War II] Tom wanted to join the army, but I think the minimum requirement was five feet and he couldn't quite make it. He went down to Sydney, and that was the last we ever heard of him. He was one of nature's gentlemen. There were plenty of people in those kind of situations, in those days.

I joined the light horse in 1937 or 1938 and had a few camps here, there and everywhere. Then after that I joined the AIF [The Australian Imperial Force] and I was in that for five years. Then I came home and worked on my father's property, got married, and then I drew a soldier settlement block and lived there for 50 years.

Six months ago, I got diagnosed with cancer. They wrote something up in some medical journal about it just recently. It said I was the oldest person in Australia (maybe anywhere) that has gone into remission. That's okay. I've lived a very long, normal and satisfying life and you can't ask any more than that.

DORIS
FROM SPRINGWOOD
BORN IN DORRIGO, 1919

NSW · 2777

I'm the second one of twin girls. My twin sister's name is Gladys. We trained together as nurses at Maitland Hospital. That was general nursing. Then we both trained at Crown Street. Midwifery. It's gone now, that hospital. It was a big place, I was sorry to see that go.

Glad and I went nursing in 1938. I had to take my grandmother's maiden name, Black, because you weren't allowed to have two nurses with the same surname. I was 18 and a half and I was so happy to get a job. Ten shillings a week—that was first year's pay—10s a week. It used to cost me 9s 6d for a packet of silk stockings, but we didn't have to pay board or keep. So that was all right. We stayed in a beautiful nurses' quarters. I remember going home and telling Mum, 'We had a lovely lunch of chops and blackberry pie, and we had maids to wait on us.'

I was at the hospital right through the war years [World War II]. We had lots of army personnel around during them years. Anyway, I finished my General before the war was over and I decided to go straight on to Crown Street and get the second certificate. I had to put my name down and wait for them to get back to me. In the meantime, the matron came into the ward one afternoon and asked me if I'd 'special' one of the doctors. He'd been in the hospital for about 12 months and he had a reputation. I said, 'No, I couldn't do that, because he's too tough. He swears at the sisters.' And she said, 'Oh, he won't swear at you!' I said, 'Yes, he would!' And I told her I couldn't do it. I was terrified of the matron, too. Anyway, I asked the matron could I go to bed and think about it, and I'd let her know tomorrow. When I think about that now, I laugh; I must have had a nerve to say that to the matron.

That night I thought, 'If I don't take the job they'll think I'm a coward.' Oh, boy! I couldn't think of anything worse. So the next day I said, 'I'll take the job, so long as he doesn't swear at me.' I must tell you this: after I started working with him, I used to put his pills on a dessertspoon and hand them to him, and I'd be standing there shaking like a leaf and the pills would be jumping up and down on the spoon. [Laughing.] I remember, he said, 'What's the matter?' I said, 'I'm terrified of you!' So he promised not to swear at me and he didn't. So we got on famously.

I married after I finished my midwifery training. He was a commissioned officer in the army. I remember the day I got married. I said to Dad, 'Walk real slow,' because I had 'nurses' back' and I was in pain. It was a nice wedding and I borrowed my cousin's wedding, so

Doris in her nurse's uniform.

> At Crown Street I did nine months in maternity.
> I didn't have a day off for nine months. I passed
> all my exams. I still have my certificates.

I was married as a proper bride. That was 1943. Didn't take me long to get pregnant, either. Bev and Robert were born in 1944.

I had twins. I broke all the rules. Most of the doctors at the hospital came to see me to tell me I'd broken all the rules. Twins are not supposed to have twins.

We married early because my husband was going to be shipped off to Burma. That's something that changes during war. You don't wait to do something, you do it 'now'. Anyway, thankfully he didn't go.

Anyway, time passed and my husband went down to Melbourne to see his people quite often and things changed—feelings changed because he was no help ... I've changed my thinking over the years. I don't think he knew how to help. He was the youngest in a big family and I think they spoilt him. Anyway, one day a sister-in-law went crook at him because he was lying on the couch while I was nursing two babies, trying to cook and trying to boil up the copper to clean nappies. She yelled at him and said, 'Get off your so and so and go and help her!'

Anyway, it didn't work and after he left I was home alone with the two kids, and one day a friend came to visit—Enis Wolfe. She asked me if I wanted a job and I said 'Yes'. Anyway, that's when the tables turned. We opened up the Bulahdelah Cottage Hospital—a big cottage hospital. We did midwifery, we did medical and we did a little bit of light surgery. Anyway, I was so pleased to have a job again, and because I could take Rob and Bev with me. I must have been there nearly 10 years.

Anyway, when I look back I've been lucky, I've been really lucky. I could always get a job. I never had a refusal. And I reared my two kids, Robert and Bev, on my own.

I was always independent. Dad even said I was too independent for my own good. I remember, I had to borrow from Dad because I'd left myself short to go home one time. Anyway, I said to him, 'I hate to ask, Dad, but can I borrow a few pounds to get home to the kids?' Anyway, I borrowed ... I can't remember if it was £5 or £10, and when I got home I posted Dad a cheque straight away. A couple of weeks later Mum wrote me a letter. She said, 'Dad got your cheque and he tore it up.' He said to her that 'Doris had never asked for anything in her life' ... and I hadn't.

I've had a good life and I've learnt that you should do what you want to do. Do it while you're young enough to do it. Because you never know from one day to another what will happen to you. If I had my life over again I'd still train as a nurse. I loved my work.

I was driving a taxi before I had a licence. Because the war was on. You got away with murder in those days. I was about 15 or 16. I remember when I turned 17 or 18, whatever age it was in those days, I went down to Katoomba Police Station. I walked in there and asked if I could get my permit. The local policeman who was there said, 'Haven't you got a licence?' He'd seen me driving around for 12 months.

NSW · 2785

ROSS
FROM BLACKHEATH
BORN IN KATOOMBA, 1924

I worked from 13 till I was 85. What's that ... a long time, I bet ya. I miss working. I miss the shop. I miss the customers.

ALLAN
FROM BRISBANE

BORN IN ROCKHAMPTON, 1927

When Dad came back from Gallipoli [after World War I], they gave him a farm. We lived 30 miles from Rockhampton. That's where I grew up with my brother and my sister.

My brother and sister went off to boarding school, but I was too wild for school. When I was 13 I went out to work on a cattle station. Up Marlborough, that's where I started off. And then I started droving on all the stations around there.

I remember the bloke in charge of the drovers, he was a black fella. And he was a terribly nice fella—I think it was Bill Hayden. I lived pretty much off the horse's back, so he used to look after me, 'cause he knew Mum and Dad real well.

I'd sleep under the stars when we drove, but back at the station we slept in a cubby house out the back. I remember the owners had two children. One was older than me and one was younger than me. I used to have to call them 'Master' and 'Mistress'. I wasn't allowed to call them by their names, Steel and Dawn. I used to sit in the kitchen on me own while they all ate in the dining room.

But I didn't mind. I loved droving. I did that—droving—for a few years, till I was about 16.

I did a bit of this and that—grader driving and 'dozer driving. Then I followed the rodeos. I wasn't a crack rider, but I had a lot of fun. One time, I seen me mate, he got a horn right through the wrist and dragged. Dragged a long way.

I went up to see him in hospital that night and the local butcher, Kevin Donnelly, was there. We all knew each other. Anyway, Kevin said to me, he said, 'Allan,' he said, 'that's where you're gunna finish up next. In a hospital bed.' I said, 'I don't know much else to do, do I?' He said, 'I'll give you a job butchering.' I said, 'Break it up! What do I know about butchering?' He said, 'I'll teach ya.' And he did. That's how I come to get into butchering.

I butchered in the area for quite a while, around Rockhampton, Gladstone and Springsure, then I bought a butcher's shop at Chermside. I was there for about seven or eight years and then I bought a butcher's shop in Newfarm in 1978. I was a butcher in Newfarm for 35 years.

ALL ROADS LEAD HOME

Ray (centre) with his brothers Ernest and Garnet in 1941. Ernest was tragically killed a few months after this picture was taken. (See page 148.)

ED FROM MANGROVE MOUNTAIN

BORN IN MELBOURNE, 1928

We came here in the period of the 'flower people', or the people who wanted to get away from Sydney and have a different lifestyle. Anne and I decided to come here because farming was in the family. It's great if you live in a community where you know a lot of the people, because there's a friendliness and a camaraderie that envelopes you.

Anne's aunt and uncle owned this property. We thought, 'Yes, this will do us.' We decided that to live on a farm was probably a good way to live, particularly for a family. I've been here 50-odd years. The crops come and go, the chooks lay well, the birds sing, the dogs bark and we are getting some frogs croaking again. Even though we have three cats that we didn't plan on, there are still a lot of birds in the trees.

And as it turned out, I've been particularly lucky, because my family have grown up, gone away and then come back. And now we all sort of work together on the farm. It's great to have not only your children but your grandchildren around, underneath your feet.

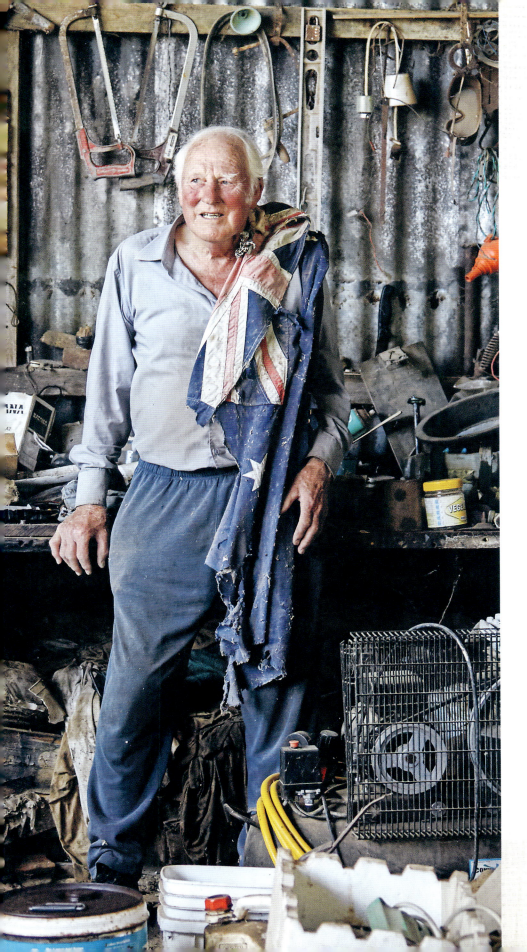

I'm a bit of a hoarder actually. When you look in the sheds, they're ready for a clean out. Always. It doesn't matter how often you clean them out, it doesn't take long to get to that stage again. Because we've got a bit of extra ground, you seem to just keep putting up extra sheds. They fill up real quick.

JIM FROM MULLUMBIMBY

NSW · 2482

BORN IN BRISBANE, 1937

It's hard to separate early memories from what you've been told. But one of my earliest ones was when my mother was up the road somewhere and I was sitting at home listening to the radio. I was probably five or six. And someone or other, I think it might have been the Jehovah's Witnesses, said that the world was predicted to end on that day. It didn't, of course, so that kind of fixed me up for predictions! It kind of turned me off prophecies of all kinds.

I grew up on the edge of Ipswich. So I could just go up the road in the bush. Most of my time, on the weekends, was spent out on the Brisbane River, a couple of Ks out on a dirt road. The beautiful Brisbane River was very clean and clear then. I used to go swimming underwater, catching little turtles. The river was my saviour in a way.

In 1970 I was 33 and living in Melbourne and my marriage fell apart. So I headed up the coast with a friend, and a few other friends from Melbourne turned up at the same time. That's how I got here. Serendipity sent me.

I think we were one of the first multiple occupancy places registered in NSW. But unlike a lot of other places, we didn't have any basic philosophy or direction. We were just heading bush and getting out of the city.

∞

To me, enlightenment is putting down your burden. Leaving your garbage behind. I think India was a big influence on me when I travelled there. It made me realise that Australia is a holy land. People thought the Aborigines were just nomads, wandering around aimlessly, but they were on pilgrimages, a lot of them. Just the same as in India.

There is so much more to discover. You don't have to go somewhere to explore. You can look down at your feet and you can start exploring there.

Everyone's happy to see women in tiny bikinis, but they're pointing to the hidden bits. But when you see people who are naked it's different. Fashion tends to sexualise the body more than nakedness.

I came to Australia at the age of 20. I came by boat. We had to get off at Sydney. I came with my parents and my little sister who was only four years old at the time. Of course, everybody used to think she was really mine. So my poor sister and I used to be labelled mother and child.

SHEILA
FROM BRISBANE
BORN IN ENGLAND, 1931

My father decided to come to Australia because there was a horrible feeling in Britain because of the Cold War. There was a lot of sabre rattling going on between America and Russia, and everybody thought Britain was going to be caught in the middle.

I'm a country boy at heart. I learnt to swim in the York swimming hole—the old river. That's where Dad had a farm. I had five brothers. You wouldn't credit it. They were scallywags, but country boys at heart. They did military service—one was in the air force, one in the army—commandos. I was the second youngest. I can recall my childhood as all good times. Great times.

⁂

Then I came down to Scotch College. They were the best years of my life, at Scotch. There were lots of scallywags. We used to get up at about four o'clock in the morning and play cricket. Cricket matches and footy matches. And I used to be a bookie—just don't tell anyone. We had a ball in those days. We became mates for life. Great mates.

BARRIE
FROM PERTH

BORN IN YORK, 1936

WA · 6011

Then, I met the love of my life, Pamela; she was about 15 years of age. My mum said, 'You're a bloody cradle snatcher!' She was a beautiful woman. I knew I'd met a good one. It was instant love. We went steady for four years and were married for 54 years. She was an incredible lady. She's gone now—dementia.

I know this might sound a little silly, but I've got my wife's ashes at home and I still buy her flowers every day. It's just love, isn't it? But life goes on.

Before I went to Scotch College I lived in Forest Street. And I used to come down and swim at Cottesloe Beach. Little did I realise back then that I would spend most of my life down here.

I was about three or four years of age when we moved from Long Gully and came into Camboon. That's where I grew up, until I was about 22 and then I shifted off—which I shouldn't have done—I should have stayed where I was.

There were nine of us. The first two children born to my mother and father were girls, and unfortunately they died very young. The oldest girl was 13 when she died. And the other one was seven. The next one to die was 22. The next one was 63. And so on. And I'm still going. I'm the only one left.

CORAL
FROM KANDOS

NSW · 2848

BORN IN LONG GULLY, 1917

I've been married twice. The first husband I met in Dubbo. I knew that he drank, but not to the extent that he did. He was just a confirmed alcoholic. He was hopeless. The drinking just got worse and worse and worse. He'd drink anything.

I had to work the whole time—after the day I married him I had to work or we would have starved. I put up with him and his drinking for so long. He eventually went and I was given sole custody of the children.

> My father never went to school. Someone once showed him a picture of the coloured coral and told him what it was. My father said it was beautiful, and he said that will be the baby's name.

I met my second husband at my second eldest daughter's home in Sydney. He was very good with the kids and he loved the grandkids. He'd pick them up of a Sunday and take them for a drive. A bit over six years I had him, before he passed away. That was 40 years ago. And I've been on my own ever since.

My son Terry, before he went to high school the teachers told me he was 'university material'. And I swore blind that whatever happened my kids would get an education. I made sure they did. I worked up until I was 72.

I had seven children. There was Norma, Janice who passed away a bit over 12 months ago, Heather, Judy, Barbara, Terry, and we named the one that died Kenneth. I lost him in Mudgee Hospital—my baby was delivered dead. I said, 'Sister, can't I just touch him? Can't I just hold him?' And she said, 'No, not in this case,' and away she went with him. He's buried in Mudgee Cemetery. A nephew of mine has put a lovely fence around him. And that's where my ashes will go.

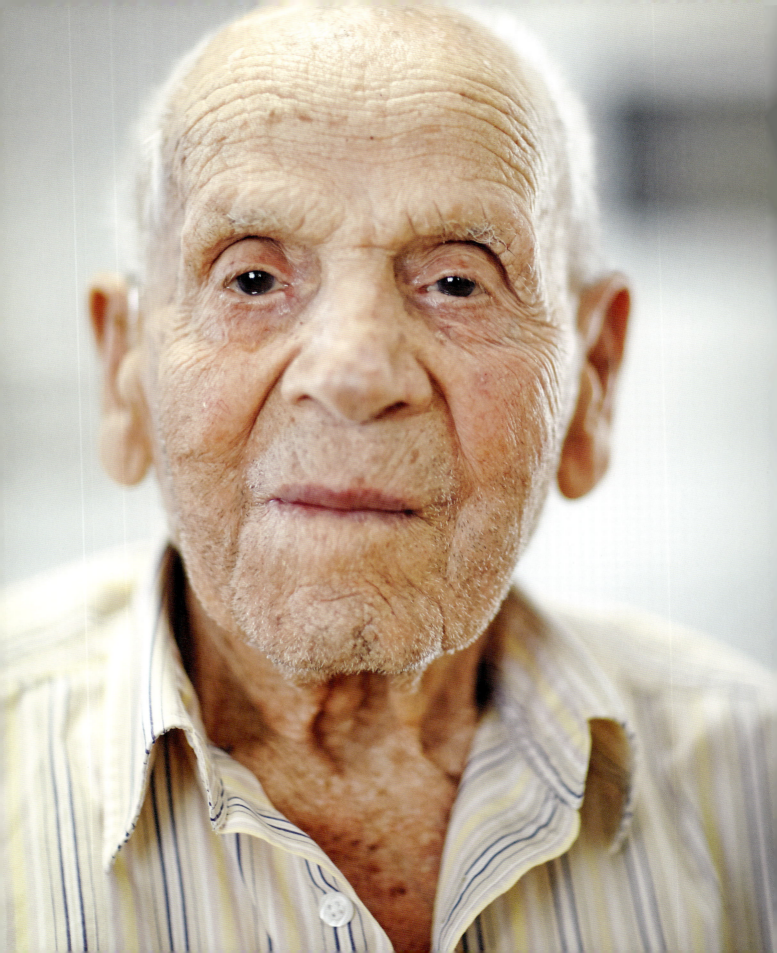

Translated from Italian to English by Giuseppe's son, Tony.

I don't remember having a toy as a child, but I do remember chasing geckos around the island [Filicudi], sometimes little snakes—not poisonous ones. That was our enjoyment, chasing little snakes and lizards. There was nothing on the island except what we could grow or catch ourselves. We grew the wheat to make the flour, to make the bread. The island was like a community and everybody helped everybody else. There was no money on the island, everybody just bartered. 'You give me fish, I give you bread.'

It was a small island, just a couple of hundred people. There was a church on the hill and everybody attended church on Saturdays and Sundays. I had 11 brothers and sisters, there were two others but they died in early childhood. I was five or six when my brothers went off to the army during the First World War. Living on the island meant we were isolated. So we didn't know much about what was going on.

Most of my days were spent fishing around the island with nets. I always enjoyed helping my father. I remember going squidding with Dad. In summer it was beautiful swimming in the crystal clear waters.

A portrait of Giuseppe, taken to impress his sweetheart, Nunziata.

GIUSEPPE
FROM PERTH

BORN IN ITALY, 1909

> The 'Don' had control of the waters in Fremantle. You had to have permission to fish in those waters. It was the Depression years, but I did alright—we got lots of lobsters—but it was not so good for other people.

⁂

I left home in November 1926 to join my brothers in Australia. Mum and Dad were very poor, they didn't have any money. So my mother's brother gave me £40 to start a new life. My dad coped with me leaving, but my mother broke down. I was 17 and she had already said goodbye to three sons. When Mum got upset, I got upset. I didn't know back then, but that was the last time I would see them.

When I arrived in Fremantle, my brothers were a thousand miles away, fishing in Shark Bay. My sponsor, Mr Paino, had a fish supply and fruit shop. He sent a worker to pick me up in a horse and cart; he took me back to the shop. While I waited for my brothers to return, I helped Mr Paino deliver fruit, vegetables and fish on the cart. When my brothers arrived back I made arrangements to go with them. We would go fishing for three weeks at a time, return to Perth for a few days, then go again.

After a few years I bought a house with my brothers. It cost £1000. The house happened to be across the road from my future wife, Nunziata. We used to talk every time we saw each other, and to make myself big I would take fish over to her family. But her father was the 'Don' of Fremantle. All the Italians would go to him for advice. Nunziata's mother was alright with me, but the Don didn't approve. Eventually, I asked him for permission and he approved. We married two years later in 1933. I was married in February and had my first child, Joe, the same year. I ended up with eight.

After the Great Depression, that's when the trouble started. When the war broke out, the government seized all our boats. Italians were interned because Italy was at war, fighting Britain. The government commandeered all our boats and towed them up river. If you weren't a naturalised Australian you were sent to prisoner of war camps. When they took my boat, I worked for a manufacturer that made boots for the soldiers, so they let me keep working and I escaped going to the camps. I didn't like Mussolini. Even though we were Italian migrants and we stuck together, the Australians treated us very well. They knew we were no threat. We were happy in Australia.

When the war finished, the government sent me a letter saying I had first option to repurchase my boat. When I went to see it, it was sunk on the river floor from years of neglect. I purchased the boat and I worked hard to fix it and start again.

My brothers and I worked harder than ever. Pulling pots, fishing and squidding and we were doing alright again—lobsters had become a commodity and everyone wanted them. I did okay in those years. Eventually, my children got involved in the fishing industry and we worked together at times.

In 1955 I had to go home, back to Italy. I hadn't been back for nearly 30 years. It was a long time. There were family problems and I had to go back to sort out my family estate. It wasn't a happy time. I also remember I had a lot of cash on me and it was a bit scary. Afterwards I went to Argentina to see my other brothers. I had a good time with them.

I retired from fishing at 60 and worked in the school garden behind my house. It seems so long ago when I think back to my childhood, when I was a boy swimming in the sea and fishing with my father.

ALLAN
FROM COCKBURN

SA · 5440

BORN IN HILLSTON, 1934

I was born in Hillston [NSW] and my daughter, what lives in Sydney, she was born in Hillston, too. I wanted one of me kids to be born in Hillston. When I was young we had to make our own fun. I had three brothers and one sister. We lived 44 miles from the nearest town on a government tank, on a hobby farm on the Lachlan River. I used to do a lot of swimming and fishing in the river back then. We used to walk five miles to school every day. It was nothing to walk five miles in those days.

My brother and I used to go bush and get the wild goats. We'd kill three or four big stinkers and salt their skin for pocket money. I loved being in the bush. Me dad used to hatch his own chickens with an incubator. He taught me how to do that also. He had chooks and turkeys, hundreds of them.

I remember one time, out on the government tank, a lot of people used to walk the roads, but this one time this bloke paraded up and down. He had riding boots on and all these marks and that. He was there for two or three days and then he disappeared. Then the police came out looking for him. Told Dad he was a murderer and he was wanted. I couldn't believe it—he'd been out the front, walking up and down.

At 14 I took on contract work, fencing. And cutting rails for shipyards. Wages wasn't much back then. I remember when I was at the sawmill, I was married with four kids and I was getting £4 10s a week.

Life's been tough. I've had two sons die and a stepson shot in the back of the head in Cabramatta. My first wife died of cancer and me sister's been gone for six years, and she was the baby.

I'm gunna sell up here, if I can, and go prospecting for gold. I had it in me hand when I was young and didn't know it. The bloke I was working for said, 'It's only silver. It's not worth nothing.' So I threw it back from where I got it from. That will be the first place I go, with my metal detector.

I'm the only one left on my side of the family, but I still got my kids. Me son rings me every other week to see if I'm okay. I'm used to living in isolation, been doing it nearly all me life.

Everything changes. It's like my tapes. I've got a thousand tapes, but now they're useless. Because every now and again they change everything. It's like the TVs, all my TVs went off a couple of months ago. I had to get them all retuned. My friend's got a big TV. It cost him seven or eight thousand. He's had it back down in Sydney getting fixed more than he's had it in his room. It keeps breaking down.

Now that's the trouble with the country, there's no one that can fix anything. See all my accordions? There's nowhere to get them fixed, because there is nowhere to take them.

All the politicians are interested in is themselves. They're supposed to be there to look after us, but they're looking after themselves. Nobody looks after me.

I learnt to play the accordion myself. See, I used to play the button accordion and the mouth organ. Me and me mate—he died here a couple of months ago, Jack Kerns from Portland—he used to play the drums. We played at weddings, engagement parties, birthday parties. We didn't get any money—we didn't ask for money—we just enjoyed playing music. We had a lot of fun at Portland, but we never made any money.

DENNIS FROM CULLEN BULLEN

BORN IN SYDNEY, 1921

NSW · 2790

I used to play every Wednesday down at the LINC in Lithgow. It's on the other side of the line. I forget what LINC stands for. See, there used to be an old dance hall—it belongs to the council—and old pensioners used to come and pay $3 for one of these takeaway meals. Anyway, 11 and a half years I was in there. And I wore a set of tyres out, no joke. I never got twopence or me name mentioned, and the bastard politicians or whatever they call themselves—councillors—they wouldn't even look at you, let alone talk to ya. They'd give a speech to the people, but they'd never thank us. We were nothing. This is what you get from the council, they couldn't care less about you. So long as you pay the rates. That's what's wrong with the country—it's gone backwards instead of forwards.

Today they've ruined the country. They give the kids dole money and they go and buy drugs with it, and then they break into someone else's place to get something to eat. That's what's wrong with the world.

They often had 'belle of the ball' and all that sort of thing. Different girls would try to see if they could get the best dress on. Everyone looked beautiful.

KATH
FROM CANN RIVER
BORN IN BENDOC, 1920

I've lived in the district my whole life. I was born in Bendoc and when I was seven we came to Chandlers Creek. There was only my brother and me on the farm. Our house was about four miles to the neighbours, that way, but even though it was isolated there was always lots of people around, somehow.

We had a big orchard and you bottled all your own fruit and made your own jam. When we'd go to the shops every fortnight, all we'd buy is flour, sugar, tea sometimes. Everything else you grew. You grew your own veggies, you killed your own meat. Mum was a good cook.

The times were good, we had lots of dances. In those days they'd have big balls—you'd go with girlfriends or a boyfriend, or sometimes a mob of you would go. They'd have the most beautiful suppers. We had a supper room outside. There was no big expense, it was all donated and volunteered. The old 4-gallon kerosene tins, they used to make coffee in one and hot water in the other. They were lovely events. It was really good. Everyone was friendly, the halls would be packed. Oh, and the music and all the suppers, they'd make all these beautiful cream sponges—because the whole valley was dairies. Yeah, you made your own fun in those days.

RAY
FROM WOODBURN
BORN IN FAULCONBRIDGE, 1920

We moved up here in 1923. Dad came here first because his brothers had brought bees up from the Blue Mountains in 1898.

Dad was a bee farmer. When I started out we were getting under 6d a pound. When the Depression was on they'd take your honey in Sydney, but they wouldn't pay you for it then. They'd pay you a penny a pound every couple of months. That's all we could get for it. I remember Dad was struggling then. That was when I was real young. But we got through it.

We had an old Chev 4 truck. In those days we'd go about 20 Ks up west from here in the forest, and we'd go out there and put up a tent and we'd extract the honey. We worked really hard back then. Dad had a thousand hives of bees at one stage—Dad and my brother and I used to work them. We worked all along the Richmond Range. In good seasons we went out west, as far as Bundarra and Inglewood, and spent the season out there.

I met me wife a couple of years after I left school. We were friends till 1943, when we got married. During the war years [World War II] they called it compulsory training and I went into camp for a month. Then they came round one morning and told me I'd been released to go to Sydney and do a course. Manpower. I worked in the munitions factory for three years during the war.

I could've got a job in Sydney after the war. I could've stopped there a while. The foreman that I worked with at the munitions factory wanted me to go with him, he was opening up a new factory, but I came back here. Dad kept onto me all throughout the war—writing me letters. He wanted me to come back and be a bee farmer. I rode me sidecar back from Sydney all loaded up, with me wife and me little dog. We settled down, had two kids. The bees bred up again quick.

When you get away from the coast it's hard to winter bees. When we came here, we had them all on the heath country during winter. They bred up quite well in those years. In the spring, we'd move to Kyogle for clover and from there back into bush on ironbark and red gum. There were three shifts in the one year.

We sent the biggest shipment of honey that ever went from here. We sent 640 tins on one boat one year. I've got a photo somewhere here. That's the biggest shipment of honey that ever left Woodburn.

We had a few hard knocks. In 1954 we had two cyclones come down here and we lost 300 hives of bees. They all drowned over on the north side of Woodburn. We couldn't get across the river. We recovered a truckload of boxes afterwards and I remember finding eight black snakes in them boxes.

We used to get bogged and all sorts of things in those early days. In 1935 we got a new Fargo truck and then in 1938 we got a new Dodge truck. That made a lot of difference. They went really well; we did a lot of miles in

A bumper season, 1954. Ray with his ex-army 1942 Diamond truck laden with a 480-gallon tank of honey.

> We arrived at Woodburn and then made our way up to Whiporie, where we had these bees; we rode in an old horse and drake. It took us two days to do the 30-odd kilometres. We lived there till 1932. Then we came back to Woodburn, and I've been here ever since.

them—the old Dodge is still down in the shed. I've had a few trucks over the years.

I remember when they shifted hives around on horse and cart. They'd move six or seven hives at a time. It had to be done after dark, 'cause you couldn't afford a bee getting out and stinging the horses. That's how Dad started out. They had an old wooden punt they used to put the horse and cart on and go across the river.

I can laugh about it now, but it wasn't funny back then. One evening, I was loading bees on the back road to Kyogle. There was a storm coming up and I was in a hurry. I got them all on except one hive, and I was racing with it on the trolley, going up the ramp, and I run in a hole and the hive fell off the trolley and burst open. The bees had been on clover, so they'd built up and were really strong.

The bees swarmed out and I grabbed the hive and had to put it back together again to get it on the truck. And I got stung from the top of me head to the bottom of me feet. They stung me through the overalls and everywhere. I'd been stung plenty of times before but nothing like this. I probably copped two or three hundred stings in one go. Eventually, I got it back together and got it strapped up and put back.

When I got in the truck I realised I could hardly feel me legs or anything. Me hands were all pins and needles and me feet were funny. Anyhow, I managed to drive to Casino. But I was just about paralysed by the time I got there. I had to unload them that night, but I couldn't do anything. I just sat on the running board for about two hours and had a thermos and a sandwich. Eventually, I got them unloaded, but I was late home for supper.

There was a lot of other bee farmers around here, but most of the old ones are all gone. My brother was a bit wiser than me. He sold his bees when he was finished with them. He sold everything he could and just retired. I've never retired. My son, Allan, is also a bee keeper, so there's always something to do around here. But my asthma is slowing me down.

JACK
FROM HERNE HILL

BORN IN PERTH, 1934

I was born in the middle of the Depression. I was an only child. Mum always said they only ever had enough money to have one.

I've been here since I was 10. My father bought the property. Mainly in those days we were growing dried fruit, which is extinct now—no one makes any money from dried fruit now.

School was only a couple of hundred metres up the road. A convent school, run by the Sisters of Mercy. First, we lived in a little rented home just near the school. I think Mum and Dad paid 7s 6d a week—that was a lot of money in those days.

Living here in the Swan Valley was like growing up in a great big village. Everyone knew each other. You had a laugh and a chat. Sport was a big thing with everyone here. I loved soccer. I reckon I had a terrific childhood. I was always happy.

When I came home from school there was always jobs to do in the vineyard. Dad would always have a list of things to do—'We'll do this, and we'll do that'—but that's the way you learnt. Now I look back and think, 'Gee, I should have learnt a lot more.' But Dad taught me a lot.

I decided to leave school at 15. Dad said, 'You need to stay at school,' but I said, 'No, I want to work in the vineyard.' He kind of succumbed to my thinking and said okay and the very first year I was home we had a bad season. We had two days and nights of strong easterly winds, which knocked all the vines and the fruit around. You only get one crop a year, so Dad says, 'This is no good, better get a job somewhere.' So we both went and worked down at Houghton Wines.

Dad wanted me to go on and become a diesel mechanic or something like that, but I wanted to stop home. I suppose farming was in me already—wanting to be on the land. It's a lifestyle choice. You've gotta love what you're doing. I like to grow things, I like to watch things grow. It's in me, so I stayed on, then Dad signed the place over to me in seventy-two or seventy-three.

> I remember when I got my first report card, they wrote that I was always of a happy disposition. And I am. That's what keeps me going through life. You know if you have a bad season, or things go wrong, you should just say, 'Oh well, next year will be better.' I think that's a big part of life—feeling content within yourself.

Back in 1951 the settlement was divided into 50 farms of about 500 acres each. A few of them were unsuccessful, most struggled. I was one of about four or five that came out well. I put that down to lots of hard work over 50 years—not trying to triple my profits every year, just improve a little each year.

After the war finished in Borneo they had a points system—so many points for overseas service and so many points if you were married. I was 25.

So I filled in a few papers about farming. My father was pretty ill at this time. He was leasing a farm at Yarra Valley and then my father died. So I worked that farm there with my mother and my younger brother for about four or five years. It was quite good, but there was no future there. So I went down to the soldier settlement to see if I could get a place. They said there's properties coming up in western Victoria, north of Port Fairy.

It was 1951, I came down with my wife, Evelyn, and had a look. One of the rules was you had to reside on your property, so on the first property the house was done, the wool shed was done, all the fencing was done. I said, 'This will do me!' So I put in for it: number one preference. Number two preference was the Stoney Rises place north of Port Fairy, which was covered in rabbits and swamps. It needed a lot of work.

WALLY
FROM PORT FAIRY
BORN IN MELBOURNE, 1923

VIC · 3284

Anyway, I got home and thought, 'By geez, I think I'm doing the wrong thing.' So I went in to see them again. I said, 'I want to swap my preferences.' I thought with a bit of hard work the Port Fairy property would be the better place. That impressed them a lot and I got it. I found out later that there were 1500 applications for the first place.

Anyway, it was a lot of hard work—there were no fences, no buildings, nothing. We came down and put huts up and lived in them for two years while the house was being built. I think I had about £700. That was my deferred payment. We stayed and farmed that land for 50 years. I was the last one to leave the soldier settlement. I was the last settler there. I couldn't have done it without Evelyn.

YVONNE
FROM YONGALA

BORN IN YONGALA, 1923

SA • 5493

My grandfather came here as the first baker in the 1880s. I wasn't around then, although sometimes I feel like I was! He came here and he had been working as a cook on the overland telephone line. There was a big mill here and because he brought all the wheat in to be made into flour, the mill people decided it would be a good profitable outlay if they had a baker. My grandfather saw that too, and so he built a bakehouse here—which is still there. He started the bakehouse in the 1890s. He brought his wife up and eventually they had a family here.

My grandfather was the baker until my father came back from the war [World War I] in 1920 and took over. It was a very lucrative business at that time. My father married in 1921. Then I was born on St Patrick's Day in 1923.

I used to help Dad deliver the bread on a horse and cart—a lovely creamy-coloured horse called Jimmy. I can remember Jimmy very well, because he was a lovely horse. I could walk in and out underneath him, giving my parents and other people heart failure.

We had lots of pets, which had come to us knocked down in the storms and so on. We had two pet galahs. One of them would take my mother's voice off. I'd be off somewhere around town and I'd hear, 'Yvonne! What are you doing? Where are you, Yvonne?' I'd come racing home to prove I was still here and I'd find out it was the cocky taking Mum off.

My sister used to get around with a doll's pram with a doll, a cat all dressed up with a bonnet and so on, and a galah all dressed up.

We had a two-sides-of-the-fence, bred-both-ways water spaniel. He was a black one. And we had a magpie that was blown down in the wind. The black dog was devoted to my father. Anyway, the magpie thought the dog was wonderful and the dog thought the magpie wasn't bad. Dad used to go up to the hotel at half past five to have a drink before it closed. And you always knew where Freddy Turner was because sitting at the front door was one black dog and one magpie.

As I say, it was a happy, happy time.

Yongala was a great community. You worked in everything—you worked at the community affairs, you worked in the sports affairs, you worked in the church affairs. You contributed to the town. We've always loved Yongala. That's how Yongala was, it was a happy town.

Now the town is dead, it hurts you very much. There's not the unity in the town that was once here. I miss that. It's like the soul has gone out of the town, however, the memories are still there.

It's a dead town at the present. But back in the 1880s until the Second World War it was a very 'go ahead' village. But with the boys going to war and the farmers buying bigger properties the town slowly declined. It's just a shell of what it used to be.

Published in 2015 by Murdoch Books,
an imprint of Allen & Unwin
Reprinted 2017

Murdoch Books Australia
83 Alexander Street
Crows Nest NSW 2065
Phone: +61 (0)2 8425 0100
Fax: +61 (0)2 9906 2218
www.murdochbooks.com.au
info@murdochbooks.com.au

Murdoch Books UK
Ormond House
26–27 Boswell Street
London WC1N 3JZ
Phone: +44 (0) 20 8785 5995
www.murdochbooks.co.uk
info@murdochbooks.co.uk

For Corporate Orders & Custom Publishing contact
Noel Hammond,
National Business Development Manager
Murdoch Books Australia

Publisher: Corinne Roberts
Design Manager: Madeleine Kane
Designer: Jacqui Triggs
Editor: Emma Hutchinson
Production Manager: Mary Bjelobrk

Text © David Darcy
The moral right of the author has been asserted.
Design © Murdoch Books 2015
Photography © David Darcy
Cover photography by David Darcy

All rights reserved. No part of this publication may be reproduced, stored in a retrieval system or transmitted in any form or by any means, electronic, mechanical, photocopying, recording or otherwise, without the prior written permission of the publisher.

A cataloguing-in-publication entry is available from the catalogue of the National Library of Australia at www.nla.gov.au.

ISBN 978 1 74336 574 8 Australia
ISBN 978 1 74336 575 5 UK

A catalogue record for this book is available from the British Library.

Colour reproduction by Splitting Image, Clayton, Victoria.
Printed by Hang Tai Printing Company Limited, China.

Cover photograph: Ed from Mangrove Mountain
Pages 2–3 photograph: Bob from Hill End
Page 4 photograph: Margaret from Kallangur

ACKNOWLEDGEMENTS

Over the past few years I've interviewed and photographed hundreds of people with their dogs for my other titles. During this time I've heard some heart-wrenching, comical and some truly inspirational stories about dogs. On occasions, some people opened up to me about other parts of their lives. These meetings, discussions and interviews have all helped nurture my growing interest in retelling life's stories. I'm grateful to everyone I've met along the way.

I would like to thank my publisher Corinne Roberts who has helped guide me over the past few years. To Dr John Skuja, thanks for going out of your way to help whilst in the Central Desert. And all the friends, family and strangers who helped me find the people in this publication.

I'd like to thank my partner Kerry who supported and shared in some of this experience with me. Thanks for riding the miles and sound-boarding ideas and thoughts.

Although my beloved dogs Felix, Eggbert and Doc will never read these words, I'm ever so grateful for the protection, loyalty and happiness they have brought to my life over the past 15 years. They are no longer able to join me on the road, but they are always on my mind. And as I write this book, they lay content and faithfully by my side.

I would also like to thank my mother, Barbara. Thanks Mum for looking after the dogs when I go away. It's always reassuring to know they are in your hands. And thanks, too, for the million other things you've done for me in this life. Love you!

David Darcy